MW01078467

Phlebotomy Vocabulary Workbook

By Lewis Morris

www.insiderswords.com/Phlebotomy

ISBN-13: 978-1694299215

Network4Learning, inc.
109 E 17th St STE 63
Cheyenne, WY 82001-4584

www.InsidersWords.com

We hope you find this vocabulary workbook helpful with your studies. If you do, please consider leaving a brief review at this link:

http://www.amazon.com/review/create-review?&asin=169429921X

Table of Contents

What is "Insider Language"?

Recent research has confirmed what we have known for decades: The strongest students and leaders in industry have a mastered an Insider Language in their subject and field. This Insider language is made up of the technical terms and vocabulary necessary to communicate effectively in classes or the workplace. For those who master it, learning is easier, faster, and much more enjoyable.

Most students who are surveyed report that the greatest challenge to any course of study is learning the vocabulary. When we examine typical college courses, we discover that there is, on average, 250 Insider Terms a student must learn over the course of a semester. Further, most exams rely heavily on this set of words for assessment purposes. The structure of multiple choice exams lends itself perfectly to the testing of this Insider Language. Students who can differentiate between Insider Language terms can handle challenging exam questions with ease and confidence.

From recent research on learning and vocabulary we have learned:

- Your knowledge of any subject is contained in the content-specific words you know. The more of these terms that you know, the easier it is to understand and recall important information; the easier it will be to communicate your ideas to peers, professors, supervisors, and co-workers. The stronger your content-area vocabulary is, the higher your scores will be on your exams and written assignments.

- Students who develop a strong Insider Language perform better on tests, learn faster, retain more information, and express greater satisfaction in learning.

- Familiarizing yourself with subject-area vocabulary before formal study (pre-learning) is the most effective way to learn this language and reap the most benefit.

- The vocabulary on standardized exams come directly from the stated objectives of the test-makers. This means that the vocabulary found on standardized exams is predictable. Our books focus on this vocabulary.

- Most multiple-choice exams are glorified vocabulary quizzes. Think about the format of a multiple-choice question. The question stem is a definition of a term and the choices (known as distractors) are 4 or 5 similar words. Your task is to differentiate between the meanings of those terms and choose the correct word.

- It takes a person several exposures to a new word to be able to use it with confidence in conversation or in writing. You need to process these words several different ways to make them part of your long-term memory.

The goals of this book are:
- To give you an "Insider Language" for your subject.
- Pre-teach the most important words before you set out on a traditional course of review or study.
- Teach you the most important words in your subject area.
- Teach you strategies for learning subject-area words on your own.
- Boost your confidence in your ability to master this language and support you in your study.
- Reduce the stress of studying and provide you with fun activities that work.

How it works:

The secret to mastering Insider Language is through repetition and exposure. We have eleven steps for you to follow:

1. Read the word and definition in the glossary out loud. "See it, Say it"
2. Identify the part of speech the word belongs to such as noun, verb, adverb, or adjective. This will help you group the word and identify similar words.
3. Place the word in context by using it in a sentence. Write this sentence down and read it aloud.
4. Use "Chunking" to group the words. Make a diagram or word cloud using these groups.
5. Make connections to the words by creating analogies.
6. Create mnemonics that help you recognize patterns and orders of words by substituting the words for more memorable items or actions.
7. Examine the morphology of the word, that is, identify the root, prefix, and suffix that make up the word. Identify similar and related words.
8. Complete word games and puzzles such as crosswords and word searches.
9. Complete matching questions that require you to differentiate between related words.
10. Complete Multiple-choice questions containing the words.
11. Create a visual metaphor or "memory cartoon" to make a mental picture of the word and related processes.

By completing this word study process, you will be exposed to the terminology in various ways that will activate your memory and create a lasting understanding of this language.

The strategies in this book are designed to make you an independent expert at learning insider language. These strategies include:

- Verbalizing the word by reading it and its definition aloud ("See It, Say It"). This allows you to make visual, auditory, and speech connections with its meaning.

- Identifying the type of word (Noun, verb, adverb, and adjective). Making this distinction helps you understand how to visualize the word. It helps you "chunk" the words into groups, and gives you clues on how to use the word.

- Place the word in context by using it in a sentence. Write this sentence down and read it aloud. This will give you an example of how the word is used.

- "Chunking". By breaking down the word list into groups of closely related words, you will learn them better and be able to remember them faster. Once you have group the terms, you can then make word clouds using a free online service. These word clouds provide visual cues to remembering the words and their meanings.

- Analogies. By creating analogies for essential words, you will be making connections that you can see on paper. These connections can trigger your memory and activate your ability to use the word in your writing as you begin to use them. Many of these analogies also use visual cues. In a sense, you can make a mental picture from the analogy.

- Mnemonics. A device such as a pattern of letters, ideas, or associations that assists in remembering something. A mnemonic is especially useful for remembering the order of a set of words or the order of a process.

- Morphology. The study of word roots, prefixes, and suffixes. By examining the structure of the words, you will gain insight into other words that are closely related, and learn how to best use the word.

- Visual metaphors. This is the most sophisticated and entertaining strategy for learning vocabulary. Create a "memory cartoon" using one or more of the vocabulary terms. This activity triggers the visual part of your memory and makes fast, permanent, imprints of the word on your memory. By combining the terms in your visual metaphor, you can "chunk" the entire set of vocabulary terms into several visual metaphors and benefit from the brain's tendency to group these terms.

The activities in this book are designed to imprint the words and their meanings in your memory in different ways. By completing each activity, you will gain the necessary exposures to the word to make it a permanent part of your vocabulary. Each activity uses a different part of your memory. The result is that you will be comfortable using these words and be able to tell the difference between closely related words. The activities include:

A. Crossword Puzzles and Word Searches- These are proven to increase test scores and improve comprehension. Students frequently report that they are fun and engaging, while requiring them to analyze the structure and meaning of the words.

B. Matching- This activity is effective because it forces you to differentiate between many closely related terms.

C. Multiple Choice- This classic question format lends itself to vocabulary study perfectly. Most exams are in this format because they are simple to make, easy to score, and are a reliable type of assessment. (Perfect for the Vocabulary Master!) One strategy to use with multiple choice questions that enhance their effectiveness is to cover the answer choices while you read the question. After reading the question, see if you can answer it before looking at the choices. Then look at the choices to see if you match one of them.

Conducting a thorough "word study" of your insider language will take time and effort, but the rewards will be well worth it. By following this guide and completing the exercises thoughtfully, you will become a stronger, more effective, and satisfied student. Best of luck on your mastery of this Insider Language!

Insider Language Strategies

"See It, Say It!" Reading your Insider Language set aloud

"IT IS BETTER TO FAIL IN ORIGINALITY THAN TO SUCCEED IN IMITATION."
-HERMAN MELVILLE

Reading aloud is the foundation for the development of an Insider Language. It is the single most important thing you can do for vocabulary acquisition. Done correctly, it engages the visual, auditory, and speech centers of the brain and hastens its storage in your long-term memory.

Reading aloud demonstrates the relationship between the printed word and its meaning.

You can read aloud on a higher level than you can initially understand, so reading aloud makes complex ideas more accessible and exposes you to vocabulary and patterns that are not part of your typical speech. Reading aloud helps you understand the complicated text better and makes more challenging text easier to grasp and understand. Reading aloud helps you to develop the "habits of mind" the strongest students use.

Reading aloud will make connections to concepts in the reading that requires you to relate the new vocabulary to things you already know. Go to the glossary at the end of this book and for each word complete the five steps outlined below:

1. Read the word and its definition aloud. Focus on the sound of the word and how it looks on the paper.
2. Read the word aloud again try to say three or four similar words; this will help you build connections to closely related words.
3. Read the word aloud a third time. Try to make a connection to something you have read or heard.
4. Visualize the concept described in the term. Paint a mental picture of the word in use.
5. Try to think of the opposite of the word. Discovering a close antonym will help you place this word in context.

Create a sentence using the word in its proper context

"OPPORTUNITIES DON'T HAPPEN. YOU CREATE THEM." –CHRIS GROSSER

Context means the circumstances that form the setting for an event, statement, or idea, and which it can be fully understood and assessed. Synonyms for context include conditions, factors, situation, background, and setting.
Place the word in context by using it in a sentence. Write this sentence down and read it aloud. By creating sentences, you are practicing using the word correctly. If you strive to make these sentences interesting and creative, they will become more memorable and effective in activating your long-term memory.

Identify the Parts of Speech
"SUCCESS IS NOT FINAL; FAILURE IS NOT FATAL: IT IS THE COURAGE TO CONTINUE THAT COUNTS." –WINSTON S. CHURCHILL

Read through each term in the glossary and make a note of what part of speech each term is. Studying and identifying parts of speech shows us how the words relate to each other. It also helps you create a visualization of each term. Below are brief descriptions of the parts of speech for you to use as a guide.

VERB: A word denoting action, occurrence, or existence. Examples: walk, hop, whisper, sweat, dribbles, feels, sleeps, drink, smile, are, is, was, has.

NOUN: A word that names a person, place, thing, idea, animal, quality, or action. Nouns are the subject of the sentence. Examples: dog, Tom, Florida, CD, pasta, hate, tiger.

ADJECTIVE: A word that modifies, qualifies, or describes nouns and pronouns. Generally, adjectives appear immediately before the words they modify. Examples: smart girl, gifted teacher, old car, red door.

ADVERB: A word that modifies verbs, adjectives and other adverbs. An "ly" ending almost always changes an adjective to an adverb. Examples: ran swiftly, worked slowly, and drifted aimlessly. Many adverbs do not end in "ly." However, all adverbs identify when, where, how, how far, how much, etc. Examples: run hot, lived hard, moved right, study smart.

Chunking

"YOUR POSITIVE ACTION COMBINED WITH POSITIVE THINKING RESULTS IN SUCCESS." SHIV KHERA

Chunking is when you take a set of words and break it down into groups based on a common relationship. Research has shown that our brains learn by chunking information. By grouping your terms, you will be able to recall large sets of these words easily. To help make your chunking go easily use an online word cloud generator to make a set of word clouds representing your chunks.

1. Study the glossary and decide how you want to chunk the set of words. You can group by part of speech, topic, letter of the alphabet, word length, etc. Try to find an easy way to group each term.
2. Once you have your different groups, visit www.wordclouds.com to create a custom word cloud for each group. Print each one of these clouds and post it in a prominent place to serve as constant visual aids for your learning.

Analogies

"CHOOSE THE POSITIVE. YOU HAVE CHOICE, YOU ARE MASTER OF YOUR ATTITUDE, CHOOSE THE POSITIVE, THE CONSTRUCTIVE. OPTIMISM IS A FAITH THAT LEADS TO SUCCESS."– BRUCE LEE

An analogy is a comparison in which an idea or a thing is compared to another thing that is quite different from it. Analogies aim at explaining an idea by comparing it to something that is familiar. Metaphors and similes are tools used to create analogies.

Analogies are useful for learning vocabulary because they require you to analyze a word (or words), and then transfer that analysis to another word. This transfer reinforces the understanding of all the words.

As you analyze the relationships between the analogies you are creating, you will begin to understand the complex relationships between the seemingly unrelated words.

_A__ is to __B_ as __C_ is to __D_

This can be written using colons in place of the terms "is to" and "as."

A:B::C:D

The two items on the left (items A & B) describe a relationship and are separated by a single colon. The two items on the right (items C & D) are shown on the right and are also separated by a colon. Together, both sides are then separated by two colons in the middle, as shown here: Tall: Short :: Skinny: Fat. The relationship used in this analogy is the antonym.

How to create an analogy

Start with the basic formula for an analogy:

_____ : _____ :: _____ : _____

Next, we will examine a simple synonym analogy:

automobile : car :: box : crate

The key to figuring out a set of word analogies is determining the relationship between the paired set of words.

Here is a list of the most common types of Analogies and examples

Synonym	Scream : Yell :: Push : Shove
Antonym	Rich : Poor :: Empty : Full
Cause is to Effect	Prosperity : Happiness :: Success : Joy
A Part is to its Whole	Toe : Foot :: Piece : Set
An Object to its Function	Car : Travel :: Read : Learn
A Item is to its Category	Tabby : House Cat :: Doberman : Dog
Word is a symptom of the other	Pain : Fracture :: Wheezing : Allergy
An object and it's description	Glass : Brittle :: Lead : Dense
The word is lacking the second word	Amputee : Limb :: Deaf : Hearing
The first word Hinders the second word	Shackles : Movement :: Stagger : Walk
The first word helps the action of the second	Knife : Bread :: Screwdriver : Screw
This word is made up of the second word	Sweater : Wool :: Jeans : Denim
A word and it's definition	Cede: Break Away :: Abolish : To get rid of

Using words from the glossary, make a set of analogies using each one. As a bonus, use more than one glossary term in a single analogy.

_____ : _____ :: _____ : _____

Name the relationship between the words in your analogy:_____

_____ : _____ :: _____ : _____

Name the relationship between the words in your analogy:_____

_____ : _____ :: _____ : _____

Name the relationship between the words in your analogy:_____

Mnemonics

"IT ISN'T THE MOUNTAINS AHEAD TO CLIMB THAT WEAR YOU OUT; IT'S THE PEBBLE IN YOUR SHOE." —MUHAMMAD ALI

A mnemonic is a learning technique that helps you retain and remember information. Mnemonics are one of the best learning methods for remembering lists or processes in order. Mnemonics make the material more meaningful by adding associations and creating patterns. Interestingly, mnemonics may work better when they utilize absurd, startling, or shocking examples and references. Mnemonics help organize the information so that you can easily retrieve it later. By giving you associations and cues, mnemonics allow you to form a mental structure ordering a list or process to help you remember it better. This mental structure allows you to create a structure of association between items that may not appear to have any relationship. Mnemonics typically use references that are easy to visualize and thus easier to remember. Through visualization of vivid images and references, the information is much easier to imprint into long-term memory. The power of making mnemonics lies in converting dull, inert and uninspiring information into something vibrant and memorable.

How to make simple and effective mnemonics
Some of the best mnemonics help us remember simple rules or lists in order.

Step 1. Take a list of terms you are trying to remember in order. For example, we will use the scientific method:

observation, question, hypothesis, methods, results, and conclusion.

Next, we will replace each word on the list with a new word that starts with the same letter. These new words will together form a vivid sentence that is easy to remember:

Objectionable Queens Haunted Macho Rednecks Creatively.

As silly as the above sentence seems, it is easy to remember, and now we can call on this sentence to remind us of the order of the scientific method.

Visit http://www.mnemonicgenerator.com/ and try typing in a list of words. It is fun to see the mnemonics that it makes and shows how easy it is to make great mnemonics to help your studying.

Using vivid words in your mnemonics allows you to see the sentence you are making. Words that are gross, scary, or name interesting animals are helpful. Profanity is also useful because the shock value can trigger memory. The following are lists of vivid words to use in your mnemonics:

Gross words

Moist, Gurgle, Phlegm, Fetus, Curd, Smear, Squirt, Chunky, Orifice, Maggots, Viscous, Queasy, Bulbous, Pustule, Putrid, Fester, Secrete, Munch, Vomit, Ooze, Dripping, Roaches, Mucus, Stink, Stank, Stunk, Slurp, Pus, Lick, Salty, Tongue, Fart, Flatulence, Hemorrhoid.

Interesting Animals

Aardvark, Baboon, Chicken, Chinchilla, Duck, Dragonfly, Emu, Electric Eel, Frog, Flamingo, Gecko, Hedgehog, Hyena, Iguana, Jackal, Jaguar, Leopard, Lynx, Minnow, Manatee, Mongoose, Neanderthal, Newt, Octopus, Oyster, Pelican, Penguin, Platypus, Quail, Racoon, Rattlesnake, Rhinoceros, Scorpion, Seahorse, Toucan, Turkey, Vulture, Weasel, Woodpecker, Yak, Zebra.

Superhero Words

Diabolical, Activate, Boom, Clutch, Dastardly, Dynamic, Dynamite, Shazam, Kaboom, Zip, Zap, Zoom, Zany, Crushing, Smashing, Exploding, Ripping, Tearing.

Scary Words

Apparition, Bat, Chill, Demon, Eerie, Fangs, Genie, Hell, Lantern, Macabre, Nightmare, Owl, Ogre, Phantasm, Repulsive, Scarecrow, Tarantula, Undead, Vampire, Wraith, Zombie.

There are several types of mnemonics that can help your memory.

1. Images

Visual mnemonics are a type of mnemonic that works by associating an image with characters or objects whose name sounds like the item that must be memorized. This is one of the easiest ways to create effective mnemonics. An example would be to use the shape of numbers to help memorize a long list of them. Numbers can be memorized by their shapes, so that: 0 -looks like an egg; 1 -a pencil, or a candle; 2 -a snake; 3 -an ear; 4 -a sailboat; 5 -a key; 6 -a comet; 7 -a knee; 8 -a snowman; 9 -a comma.

Another type of visual mnemonic is the word-length mnemonic in which the number of letters in each word corresponds to a digit. This simple mnemonic gives pi to seven decimal places:

3.141582 becomes "How I wish I could calculate pi."

Of course, you could use this type of mnemonic to create a longer sentence showing the digits of an important number. Some people have used this type of mnemonic to memorize thousands of digits.

Using the hands is also an important tool for creating visual objects. Making the hands into specific shapes can help us remember the pattern of things or the order of a list of things.

2. Rhyming

Rhyming mnemonics are quick ways to make things memorable. A classic example is a mnemonic for the number of days in each month:
"30 days hath September, April, June, and November.
All the rest have 31
Except February, my dear son.
It has 28, and that is fine
But in Leap Year it has 29."

Another example of a rhyming mnemonic is a common spelling rule:
"I before e except after c
or when sounding like a
in neighbor and weigh."

Use **rhymer.com** to get large lists of rhyming words.

3. Homonym

A homonym is one of a group of words that share the same pronunciation but have different meanings, whether spelled the same or not.

Try saying what you're attempting to remember out loud or very quickly, and see if anything leaps out. If you know other languages, using similar-sounding words from those can be effective.

You could also browse this list of homonyms
at http://www.cooper.com/alan/homonym_list.html.

4. Onomatopoeia

An Onomatopeia is a word that phonetically imitates, resembles or suggests the source of the sound that it describes. Are there any noises made by the thing you're trying to memorize? Is it often associated with some other sound? Failing that, just make up a noise that seems to fit.

Achoo, ahem, baa, bam, bark, beep, beep beep, belch, bleat, boo, boo hoo, boom, burp, buzz, chirp, click clack, crash, croak, crunch, cuckoo, dash, drip, ding dong, eek, fizz, flit, flutter, gasp, grrr, ha ha, hee hee, hiccup, hiss, hissing, honk, icky, itchy, jiggly, jangle, knock knock, lush, la la la, mash, meow, moan, murmur, neigh, oink, ouch, plop, pow, quack, quick, rapping, rattle, ribbit, roar, rumble, rustle, scratch, sizzle, skittering, snap crackle pop, splash, splish splash, spurt, swish, swoosh, tap, tapping, tick tock, tinkle, tweet, ugh, vroom, wham, whinny, whip, whooping, woof.

5. Acronyms

An acronym is a word or name formed as an abbreviation from the initial components of a word, such as NATO, which stands for North Atlantic Treaty Organization. If you're trying to memorize something involving letters, this is often a good bet. A lot of famous mnemonics are acronyms, such as ROYGBIV which stands for the order of colors in the light spectrum (Red, Orange, Yellow, Green, Blue, Indigo, and Violet).
A great acronym generator to try is: www.all-acronyms.com.

A different spin on an acronym is a backronym. A **backronym** is a specially constructed phrase that is supposed to be the source of a word that is an acronym. A backronym is constructed by creating a new phrase to fit an already existing word, name, or acronym.

The word is a combination of *backward* and *acronym*, and has been defined as a "reverse acronym." For example, the United States Department of Justice assigns to their Amber Alert program the meaning "**A**merica's **M**issing: **B**roadcast **E**mergency **R**esponse." The process can go either way to make good mnemonics.

Visit: https://arthurdick.com/projects/backronym/ to try out a simple backronym generator.

6. Anagrams

An anagram is a direct word switch or word play, the result of rearranging the letters of a word or phrase to produce a new word or phrase, using all the original letters exactly once; for example, the word anagram can be rearranged into nag-a-ram.

Try re-arranging letters or components and see if anything memorable emerges. Visit http://www.nameacronym.net/ to use a simple anagram generator.

One particularly memorable form of anagram is the spoonerism, where you swap the initial syllables or letters of words to make new phrases. These are usually humorous, and this makes them easier to remember. Here are some examples:

"Is it kisstomary to cuss the bride?" (as opposed to "customary to kiss")
"The Lord is a shoving leopard." (instead of "a loving shepherd")
"A blushing crow." ("crushing blow")
"A well-boiled icicle" ("well-oiled bicycle")
"You were fighting a liar in the quadrangle." ("lighting a fire")
"Is the bean dizzy?" (as opposed to "is the dean busy?")

7. Stories

Make up quick stories or incidents involving the material you want to memorize. For larger chunks of information, the stories can get more elaborate. Structured stories are particularly good for remembering lists or other sequenced information. Have a look at https://en.wikipedia.org/wiki/Method_of_loci for a more advanced memory sequencing technique.

Visual Metaphors

"LIMITS, LIKE FEAR, IS OFTEN AN ILLUSION." –MICHAEL JORDAN

What is a Metaphor?

A metaphor is a figure of speech that refers to one thing by mentioning another thing. Metaphors provide clarity and identify hidden similarities between two seemingly unrelated ideas. A visual metaphor is an image that creates a link between different ideas.

Visual metaphors help us use our understanding of the world to learn new concepts, skills, and ideas. Visual metaphors help us relate new material to what we already know. Visual metaphors must be clear and simple enough to spark a connection and understanding. Visual metaphors should use familiar things to help you be less fearful of new, complex, or challenging topics. Metaphors trigger a sense of familiarity so that you are more accepting of the new idea. Metaphors work best when you associate a familiar, easy to understand idea with a challenging, obscure, or abstract concept.

How to make a visual metaphor

1. Brainstorm using the words of the concept. Use different fonts, colors, or shapes to represent parts of the concept.

2. Merge these images together

3. Show the process using arrows, accents, etc.

4. Think about the story line your metaphor projects.

Examples of visual metaphors:

A skeleton used to show a framework of something.

A cloud showing an outline.

A bodybuilder whose muscles represent supporting ideas and details.

A sandwich where the meat, tomato, and lettuce represent supporting ideas.

A recipe card to show a process.

Your metaphor should be accurate. It should be complex enough to convey meaning, but simple and clear enough to be easily understood.

Morphology
"SCIENCE IS THE CAPTAIN, AND PRACTICE THE SOLDIERS." LEONARDO DA VINCI

Morphology is the study of the origin, roots, suffixes, and prefixes of the words. Understanding the meaning of prefixes, suffixes, and roots make it easier to decode the meaning of new vocabulary. Having the ability to decode using morphology increases text comprehension when initially reading as well.

The capability of identifying meaningful parts of words (morphemes), including prefixes, suffixes, and roots can be helpful. Identifying morphemes improves decoding accuracy and fluency. Reading speed improves when you can decode larger chunks of text quickly. When you can recognize morphemes in words, you will be better able to make sense of new words in context. Below are charts containing the most common prefixes, suffixes, and root words. Use them to help you decode your vocabulary terms.

Prefixes

Prefix	Meaning	Example words and meanings	
a, ab, abs	away from	absent abdicate	not to be present, to give up an office or throne.
ad, a, ac, af, ag, an, ar, at, as	to, toward	Advance advantage	To move forward To have the upper hand
anti	against	Antidote antisocial antibiotic	To repair poisoning refers to someone who's not social
bi, bis	two	bicycle binary biweekly	two-wheeled cycle two number system every two weeks
circum, cir	around	circumnavigate circle	Travel around the world a figure that goes all around
com, con, co, col	with, together	Complete Complement	To finish To go along with
de	away from, down, the opposite of	depart detour	to go away from to go out of your way
dis, dif, di	apart	dislike dishonest distant	not to like not honest away
En-, em-	Cause to	Entrance	the way in.
epi	upon, on top of	epitaph epilogue epidemic	writing upon a tombstone speech at the end, on top of the rest
equ, equi	equal	equalize equitable	to make equal fair, equal
ex, e, ef	out, from	exit eject exhale	to go out to throw out to breathe out
Fore-	Before	Forewarned	To have prior warning

Prefix	Meaning	Example Words and Meanings	
in, il, ir, im, en	in, into	Infield Imbibe	The inner playing field to take part in
in, il, ig, ir, im	not	inactive ignorant irreversible irritate	not active not knowing not reversible to put into discomfort
inter	between, among	international interact	among nations to mix with
mal, male	bad, ill, wrong	malpractice malfunction	bad practice fail to function, bad function
Mid	Middle	Amidships	In the middle of a ship
mis	wrong, badly	misnomer	The wrong name
mono	one, alone, single	monocle	one lensed glasses
non	not, the reverse of	nonprofit	not making a profit
ob	in front, against, in front of, in the way of	Obsolete	No longer needed
omni	everywhere, all	omnipresent omnipotent	always present, everywhere all powerful
Over	On top	Overdose	Take too much medication
Pre	Before	Preview	Happens before a show.
per	through	Permeable pervasive	to pass through, all encompassing
poly	many	Polygamy polygon	many spouses figure with many sides
post	after	postpone postmortem	to do after after death
pre	before, earlier than	Predict Preview	To know before To view before release
pro	forward, going ahead of, supporting	proceed pro-war promote	to go forward supporting the war to raise or move forward
re	again, back	retell recall reverse	to tell again to call back to go back
se	apart	secede seclude	to withdraw, become apart to stay apart from others
Semi	Half	Semipermeable	Half-permeable

Prefix	Meaning	Example Words and Meanings	
Sub	under, less than	Submarine	under water
super	over, above, greater	superstar superimpose	a start greater than her stars to put over something else
trans	across	transcontinental transverse	across the continent to lie or go across
un, uni	one	unidirectional unanimous unilateral	having one direction sharing one view having one side
un	not	uninterested unhelpful unethical	not interested not helpful not ethical

Roots

Root	Meaning	Example words & meanings	
act, ag	to do, to act	Agent Activity	One who acts as a representative Action
Aqua	Water	Aquamarine	The color of water
Aud	To hear	Auditorium	A place to hear music
apert	open	Aperture	An opening
bas	low	Basement Basement	Something that is low, at the bottom A room that is low
Bio	Living thing	Biological	Living matter
cap, capt, cip, cept, ceive	to take, to hold, to seize	Captive Receive Capable Recipient	One who is held To take Able to take hold of things One who takes hold or receives
ced, cede, ceed, cess	to go, to give in	Precede Access Proceed	To go before Means of going to To go forward
Cogn	Know	Cognitive	Ability to think
cred, credit	to believe	Credible Incredible Credit	Believable Not believable Belief, trust
curr, curs, cours	to run	Current Precursory Recourse	Now in progress, running Running (going) before To run for aid
Cycle	Circle	Lifecycle	The circle of life
dic, dict	to say	Dictionary Indict	A book explaining words (sayings)

Root	Meaning	Examples and meanings	
duc, duct	to lead	Induce Conduct Aqueduct	To lead to action To lead or guide Pipe that leads water somewhere
equ	equal, even	Equality Equanimity	Equal in social, political rights Evenness of mind, tranquility
fac, fact, fic, fect, fy	to make, to do	Facile Fiction Factory Affect	Easy to do Something that is made up Place that makes things To make a change in
fer, ferr	to carry, bring	Defer Referral	To carry away Bring a source for help/information
Gen	Birth	Generate	To create something
graph	write	Monograph Graphite	A writing on a particular subject A form of carbon used for writing
Loc	Place	Location	A place
Mater	Mother	Maternity	Expecting birth
Mem	Recall	Memory	The recall experiences
mit, mis	to send	Admit Missile	To send in Something sent through the air
Nat	Born	Native	Born in a place
par	equal	Parity Disparate	Equality No equal, not alike
Ped	Foot	Podiatrist	Foot doctor
Photo	Light	Photograph	A picture
plic	to fold, to bend, to turn	Complicate Implicate	To fold (mix) together To fold in, to involve
pon, pos, posit, pose	to place	Component Transpose Compose Deposit	A part placed together with others A place across To put many parts into place To place for safekeeping
scrib, script	to write	Describe Transcript Subscription	To write about or tell about A written copy A written signature or document
sequ, secu	to follow	Sequence	In following order

Root	Meaning	Examples and Meanings	
Sign	Mark	Signal	to alert somebody
spec, spect, spic	to appear, to look, to see	Specimen Aspect	An example to look at One way to see something
sta, stat, sist,	to stand, or make stand	Constant	Standing with
stit, sisto	Stable, steady	Status Stable Desist	Social standing Steady (standing) To stand away from
Struct	To build	Construction	To build a thing
tact	to touch	Contact Tactile	To touch together To be able to be touched
ten, tent, tain	to hold	Tenable Retentive Maintain	Able to be held, holding Holding To keep or hold up
tend, tens, tent	to stretch	Extend Tension	To stretch or draw out Stretched
Therm	Temperature	Thermometer	Detects temperature
tract	to draw	Attract Contract	To draw together An agreement drawn up
ven, vent	to come	Convene Advent	To come together A coming
Vis	See	Invisible	Cannot be seen
ver, vert, vers	to turn	Avert Revert Reverse	To turn away To turn back To turn around

Crossword Puzzles

1. *Using the Across and Down clues, write the correct words in the numbered grid below.*

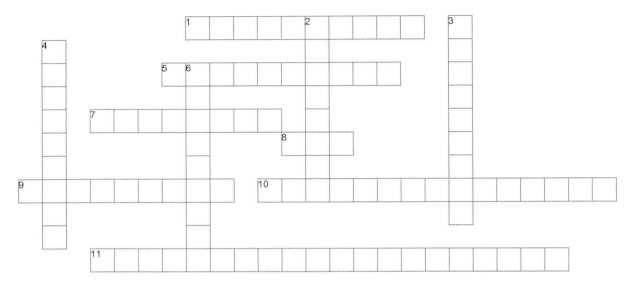

ACROSS

1. An organ or tissue taken from the body for grafting into another part of the same body or into another individual.

5. An inherited feature on the surface of the red blood cell. A series of related blood groups make up a blood group system such as the ABO system or the Rh system.

7. Pertaining to or composed of blood vessels. The vascular system is composed of the heart, blood vessels, lymphatics and their parts considered collectively.

8. Human Immunodeficiency Virus

9. Relative to venipunctures, the appearance of a small amount of blood in the neck of a syringe or the tubing of a butterfly. This is a sign that the vein has been properly accessed.

10. Safety cabinets with air flow in such a direction as to carry any harmful materials or fumes away from the worker.

11. A set of procedures and protocols designed to protect the healthcare worker which uses the basic concept that each patient must be treated as though they were infected with an infectious disease.

DOWN

2. A thin film of paraffin used primarily in the laboratory to seal open containers such as test tubes.

3. A small needle with two plastic wings attached which are squeezed together to form a tab that is used to manipulate the needle.

4. The conversion of blood from a liquid form to solid through the process of coagulation.

6. White blood cells.

A. Vascular
D. Universal Precautions
G. Parafilm
J. Leukocyte

B. HIV
E. Butterfly
H. Blood group
K. Flash back

C. Blood clot
F. Laminar flow hood
I. Transplant

2. Using the Across and Down clues, write the correct words in the numbered grid below.

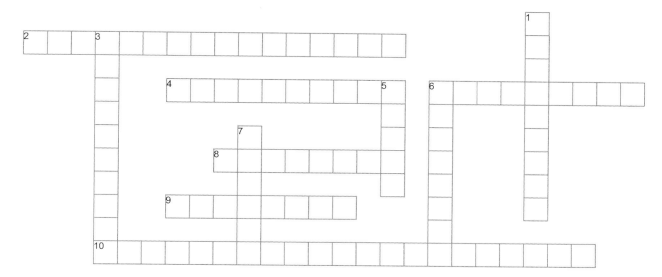

ACROSS

2. That part of the arm opposing the elbow.
4. The state of the body early in the morning, approximately 12 hours after the last ingestion of food or other nutrition.
6. Any one of the minute vessels that connect the arterioles and venules, forming a network in nearly all parts of the body.
8. A thin film of paraffin used primarily in the laboratory to seal open containers such as test tubes.
9. The process of cleansing the blood by passing it through a special machine. Dialysis is necessary when the kidneys are not able to filter the blood.
10. Average volume of red blood cells.

DOWN

1. An outflow, usually of fluid.
3. The outside layer of cells that covers all the free, open surfaces of the body including the skin, and mucous membranes that communicate with the outside of the body.
5. The swelling of soft tissues caused by excess fluid accumulation.
6. A thin, flexible tube. When a catheter is placed in a vein, it provides a pathway for giving drugs, nutrients, fluids, or blood products.
7. Paleness; decrease of absence of skin color.

A. Capillary
D. Dialysis
G. Epithelium
J. Basal state

B. Antecubital fossa
E. Parafilm
H. Pallor
K. Effluent

C. Catheter
F. Edema
I. Mean Corpuscular Volume

3. *Using the Across and Down clues, write the correct words in the numbered grid below.*

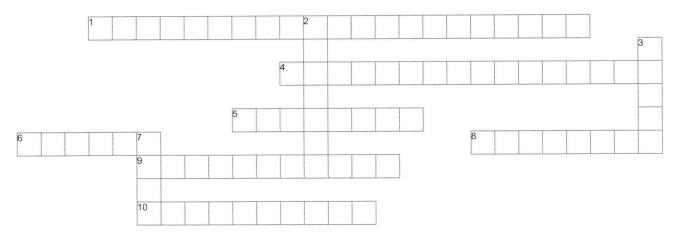

ACROSS

1. Average volume of red blood cells.

4. That part of the arm opposing the elbow.

5. One of the minute particles seen with the electron microscope in many types of cells, containing various hydrolytic enzymes and normally involved in the process of localized digestion inside the cell.

6. A bruise or ""contusion" is a traumatic injury of the soft tissues which results in breakage of the local capillaries and leakage of red blood cells.

8. As it relates to blood drawing, the material that is withdrawn with a negative pressure apparatus (syringe).

9. Formation of profuse perspiration (sweat). A symptom of syncope or vasovagal response.

10. A drug that causes unconsciousness or a loss of general sensation. A local anesthetic causes loss of feeling in a part of the body.

DOWN

2. Fainting; a temporary loss of consciousness due to a reduction of blood to the brain.

3. Needle diameter is measured by gauge; the larger the needle diameter, the smaller the gauge.

7. A calcium chelating (binding) agent that is used as an anticoagulant for laboratory blood specimens. Also used in treatment of lead poisoning.

A. Gauge
D. Antecubital fossa
G. Lysosome
J. Syncope

B. EDTA
E. Mean Corpuscular Volume
H. Anesthetic

C. Aspirate
F. Bruise
I. Diaphoretic

4. Using the Across and Down clues, write the correct words in the numbered grid below.

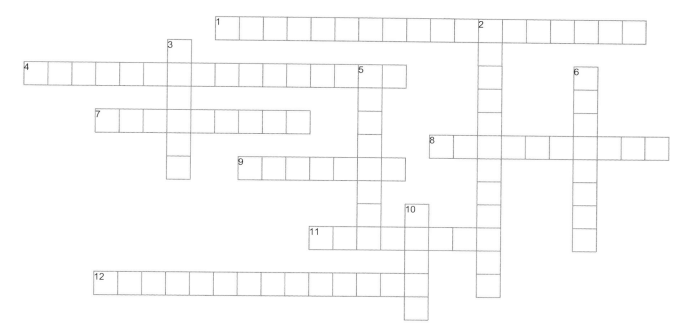

ACROSS

1. Controls (e.g., sharps disposal containers, self-sheathing needles) that isolate or remove the bloodborne pathogens hazard from the workplace.

4. A group or series of enzymatic reactions in living aerobic organisms that results in the production of energy.

7. An agent that kills pathogenic microorganisms

8. The incision of a vein as for blood-letting (venesection); needle puncture of a vein for drawing blood (venipuncture).

9. Outside the living body; inside a glass; observable in a test tube.

11. A popular tradename iodine-containing topical antiseptic agent; povidone-iodine.

12. The sodium salt of warfarin, one of the synthetic anticoagulants. Coumadin is a brand name.

DOWN

2. A large vein of the arm that empties into the axillary vein

3. Referring to the palm surface or side of the hand

5. Carrying away. An artery is an efferent vessel carrying blood away from the heart.

6. Also known as a thrombocyte, this is a particulate component of the blood known for its involvement in blood coagulation.

10. The swelling of soft tissues caused by excess fluid accumulation.

A. Citric Acid Cycle	B. Betadine	C. Edema	D. Warfarin sodium
E. Phlebotomy	F. Platelet	G. Invitro	H. Engineering control
I. Efferent	J. Cephalic vein	K. Germicide	L. Palmar

5. *Using the Across and Down clues, write the correct words in the numbered grid below.*

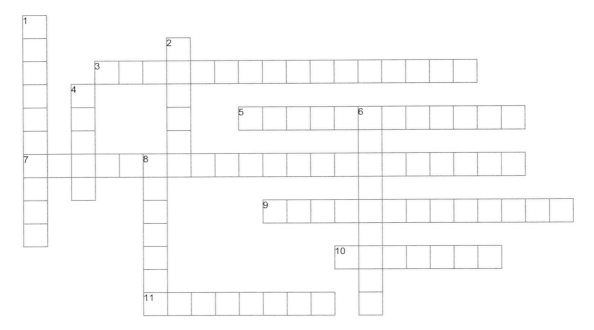

ACROSS

3. Enclosed containers used to hold specimen tubes for centrifugation.

5. A test which involves the incubation of a blood specimen overnight to determine if bacteria are present.

7. Small, flexible plastic tube inserted into the large vein above the heart, through which drugs and blood products can be given and blood samples withdrawn painlessly.

9. A type of an arteriovenous fistula consisting of either a venous autograft or synthetic tube which is grafted to the artery and vein.

10. To examine or feel by the hand. In relation to venipunctures, this technique is used to "feel" a vein which will tend to rebound when slight pressure is applied with the finger.

11. A thin, flexible tube. When a catheter is placed in a vein, it provides a pathway for giving drugs, nutrients, fluids, or blood products.

DOWN

1. Any of the mononuclear, nonphagocytic leukocytes, found in the blood and lymph, which are the body's immunologically competent cells.

2. Denoting a position more toward the back surface than some other object of reference; same as posterior in human anatomy.

4. A sudden loss of consciousness.

6. The process of clot formation. Part of an important host defense mechanism call hemostasis.

8. Having molecular oxygen present.

A. Aerobic
D. Palpate
G. Vascular graft
J. Catheter

B. Coagulate
E. Blood culture
H. Faint
K. Central venous catheter

C. Lymphocyte
F. Dorsal
I. Aerosol canisters

6. *Using the Across and Down clues, write the correct words in the numbered grid below.*

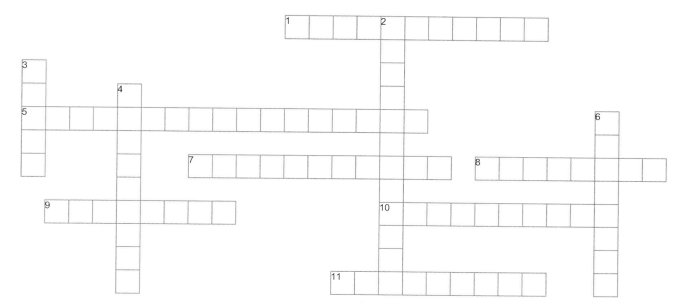

ACROSS

1. All the vessels lined with endothelium through which blood circulates.
5. Medications that, like aspirin, reduce the tendency of platelets in the blood to clump and clot.
7. A cell containing but one nucleus. In blood circulation, monocyte and lymphocyte.
8. Nearest to any other point of reference.
9. Toward the front or in front of.
10. A constrictive band, placed over an extremity to distend veins for blood aspiration or intravenous injections.
11. A small needle with two plastic wings attached which are squeezed together to form a tab that is used to manipulate the needle.

DOWN

2. An agent that disinfects, applied particularly to agents used on inanimate objects.
3. An implant or transplant of any tissue or organ.
4. A technique in which blood products are separated from a donor and the desired elements collected and the rest returned to the donor.
6. A localized collection of blood within tissue due to leakage from the wall of a blood vessel, producing a bluish discoloration (ecchymosis)and pain.

A. Disinfectant   B. Tourniquet   C. Antiplatelet agent   D. Hematoma
E. Butterfly   F. Apheresis   G. Graft   H. Blood vessel
I. Mononuclear   J. Proximal   K. Anterior

7. *Using the Across and Down clues, write the correct words in the numbered grid below.*

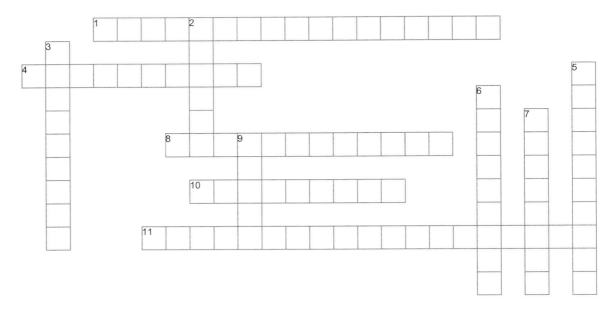

ACROSS

1. Blood which has been deprived of fibrin.
4. The determination of the proper number of red blood cells, white blood cells and platelets are present in the patient's blood.
8. The component of the blood that contains hemoglobin which is responsible for oxygen and carbon dioxide exchange.
10. The conversion of blood from a liquid form to solid through the process of coagulation.
11. Precautions that are designed for the care of all patients in hospitals regardless of their diagnosis or presumed infection status.

DOWN

2. A bruise or ""contusion" is a traumatic injury of the soft tissues which results in breakage of the local capillaries and leakage of red blood cells.
3. Relative to venipunctures, the appearance of a small amount of blood in the neck of a syringe or the tubing of a butterfly. This is a sign that the vein has been properly accessed.
5. The formation of a blood clot (thrombus) within a vessel.
6. Inflammation of a vein. The condition is marked by infiltration of the layers of the vein and the formation of a clot. It produces edema, stiffness and pain in the affected area.
7. A localized collection of blood within tissue due to leakage from the wall of a blood vessel, producing a bluish discoloration (ecchymosis)and pain.
9. The fluid in the body that contains red cells and white cells as well as platelets, proteins, plasma and other elements. It is transported throughout the body by the Circulatory System.

A. Phlebitis
E. Blood count
I. Hematoma
B. Blood clot
F. Thrombosis
J. Standard Precautions
C. Bruise
G. Blood
K. Cefibrinated blood
D. Flash back
H. Red blood cell

8. *Using the Across and Down clues, write the correct words in the numbered grid below.*

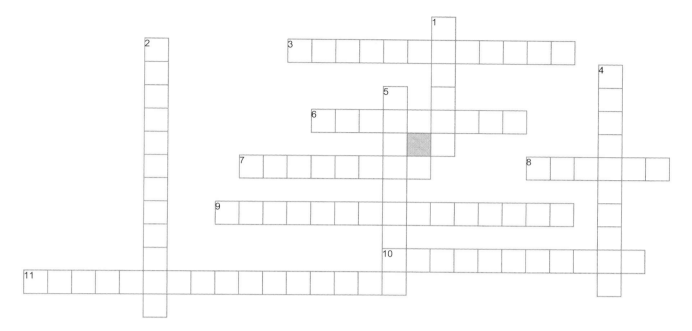

ACROSS

3. The science concerned with the study of factors influencing the distribution of disease and their causes in a defined population.

6. A small branch of an artery that leads to a capillary. Also, see capillary.

7. One of the minute particles seen with the electron microscope in many types of cells, containing various hydrolytic enzymes and normally involved in the process of localized digestion inside the cell.

8. Denoting a position more toward the back surface than some other object of reference; same as posterior in human anatomy.

9. A hollow silicone (soft, rubber-like material) tube inserted and secured into a large vein in the chest for long-term use to administer drugs or nutrients.

10. Formation of profuse perspiration (sweat). A symptom of syncope or vasovagal response.

11. A method used by microbiologists and clinicians to keep cultures, sterile instruments and media, and people free of microbial contamination.

DOWN

1. The protein formed during normal blood clotting that is the essence of the clot.

2. A process where polymorphonuclear leukocytes, monocytes, and macrophages combine with lysosomes within the cell cytoplasm to digest and destroy a particulate.

4. Something that discourages the growth microorganisms. By contrast, aseptic refers to the absence of microorganisms.

5. An agent that kills pathogenic microorganisms

A. Arteriole
E. Lysosome
I. Fibrin

B. Epidemiology
F. Dorsal
J. Aseptic technique

C. Diaphoretic
G. Hickman catheter
K. Phagocytosis

D. Germicide
H. Antiseptic

9. *Using the Across and Down clues, write the correct words in the numbered grid below.*

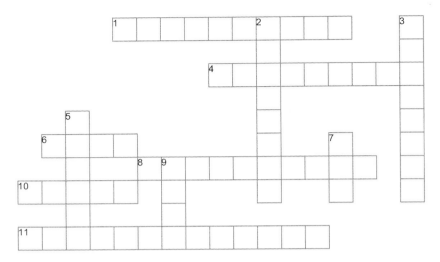

ACROSS

1. An eosin (red) staining leukocyte with a nucleus that usually has two lobes connected by a slender thread of chromatin, and cytoplasm containing coarse, round granules that are uniform in size.

4. The more readily stainable portion of the cell nucleus. It is a DNA attached to a protein structure and is the carrier of genes in inheritance.

6. Blood vessels carrying blood to the heart. Blood contained within these vessels is generally bound with carbon dioxide which will be exchanged for oxygen in the lungs.

8. The oxygen carrying pigment of the red blood cells.

10. Lying face down; opposed to supine.

11. A type of an arteriovenous fistula consisting of either a venous autograft or synthetic tube which is grafted to the artery and vein.

DOWN

2. A thin film of paraffin used primarily in the laboratory to seal open containers such as test tubes.

3. A mononuclear, phagocytic leukocyte.

5. Pertaining to the veins, or blood passing through them.

7. Human Immunodeficiency Virus

9. A calcium chelating (binding) agent that is used as an anticoagulant for laboratory blood specimens. Also used in treatment of lead poisoning.

A. Eosinophil
B. Vascular graft
C. Vein
D. Chromatin
E. Venous
F. Prone
G. HIV
H. Monocyte
I. EDTA
J. Hemoglobin
K. Parafilm

10. *Using the Across and Down clues, write the correct words in the numbered grid below.*

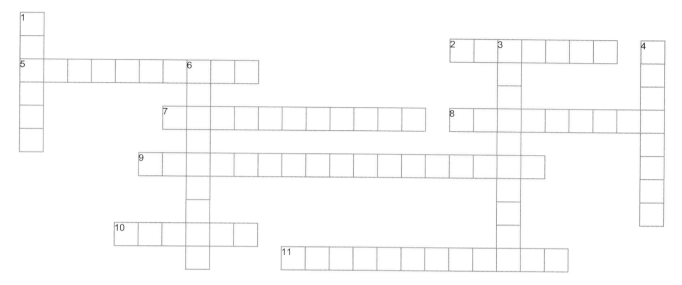

ACROSS

2. A compound that is an intermediate in the citric acid cycle (Krebs cycle or glycolysis). Citrate chelates (binds) calcium ions, preventing blood clotting and, thus, is an effective anticoagulant.

5. The skin discoloration caused by a bruise (contusion).

7. All the vessels lined with endothelium through which blood circulates.

8. An agent that kills pathogenic microorganisms

9. Hemoglobin which has been bound with carbon monoxide, which has an affinity for hemoglobin 200 times greater than oxygen.

10. Inside the living body.

11. Also known as a platelet, this is a particulate component of the blood, approximately 2-4 microns in diameter and known for its involvement in blood coagulation.

DOWN

1. The condition of having less than the normal number of red blood cells or hemoglobin in the blood.

3. A constrictive band, placed over an extremity to distend veins for blood aspiration or intravenous injections.

4. Toward the front or in front of.

6. A hardening, especially from inflammation and certain disease states. Though sclerosis may occur in many areas of the body, the term is most often associated with blood vessels.

A. Invivo   B. Anterior   C. Blood vessel   D. Germicide
E. Ecchymosis   F. Sclerosis   G. Carboxyhemoglobin   H. Anemia
I. Tourniquet   J. Thrombocyte   K. Citrate

11. *Using the Across and Down clues, write the correct words in the numbered grid below.*

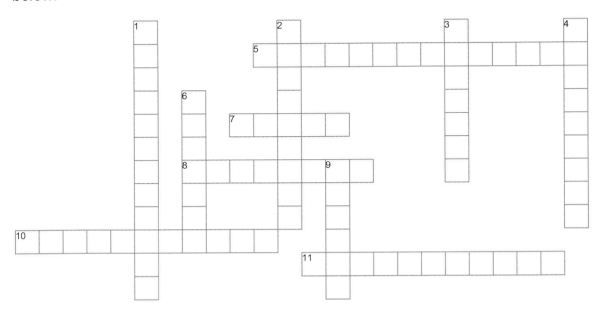

ACROSS

5. Used as a topical antiseptic, this is a compound made by reacting iodine with povidone which slowly releases iodine.

7. Of short duration. Rapid and abbreviated in onset.

8. Nearest to any other point of reference.

10. Formation of profuse perspiration (sweat). A symptom of syncope or vasovagal response.

11. A preventative treatment.

DOWN

1. The science concerned with the study of factors influencing the distribution of disease and their causes in a defined population.

2. A bruise or injury without a break in the skin.

3. An abnormal passageway usually between two internal organs. Such passages may be created experimentally for obtaining body secretions for study.

4. An agent that kills pathogenic microorganisms

6. To examine or feel by the hand. In relation to venipunctures, this technique is used to "feel" a vein which will tend to rebound when slight pressure is applied with the finger.

9. To suck up, as through pores.

A. Palpate
E. Povidone iodine
I. Diaphoretic

B. Proximal
F. Prophylaxis
J. Absorb

C. Germicide
G. Acute
K. Epidemiology

D. Fistula
H. Contusion

12. *Using the Across and Down clues, write the correct words in the numbered grid below.*

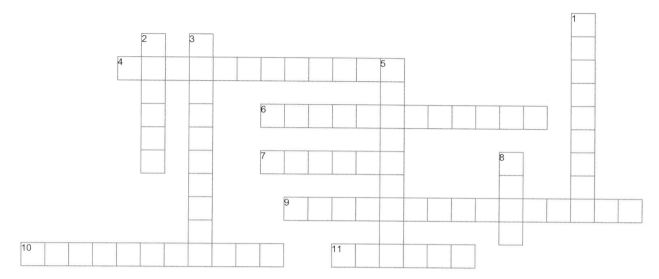

ACROSS

4. A test which involves the incubation of a blood specimen overnight to determine if bacteria are present.

6. A test which measures the time it takes for small blood vessels to close off and bleeding to stop.

7. A bruise or ""contusion" is a traumatic injury of the soft tissues which results in breakage of the local capillaries and leakage of red blood cells.

9. A hollow silicone (soft, rubber-like material) tube inserted and secured into a large vein in the chest for long-term use to administer drugs or nutrients.

10. The layer of cells lining the closed internal spaces of the body such as the blood vessels and lymphatic vessels.

11. To attract and retain other material on the surface.

DOWN

1. The conversion of blood from a liquid form to solid through the process of coagulation.

2. The fluid portion of the blood in which the cellular components are suspended. Plasma contains coagulation factors used in the clotting of blood as opposed to serum.

3. An eosin (red) staining leukocyte with a nucleus that usually has two lobes connected by a slender thread of chromatin, and cytoplasm containing coarse, round granules that are uniform in size.

5. The upper or outer layer of the two main layers of cells that make up the skin.

8. A calcium chelating (binding) agent that is used as an anticoagulant for laboratory blood specimens. Also used in treatment of lead poisoning.

A. Epidermis	B. Plasma	C. Bleeding time	D. Blood clot
E. Adsorb	F. Hickman catheter	G. Eosinophil	H. EDTA
I. Bruise	J. Blood culture	K. Endothelium	

13. *Using the Across and Down clues, write the correct words in the numbered grid below.*

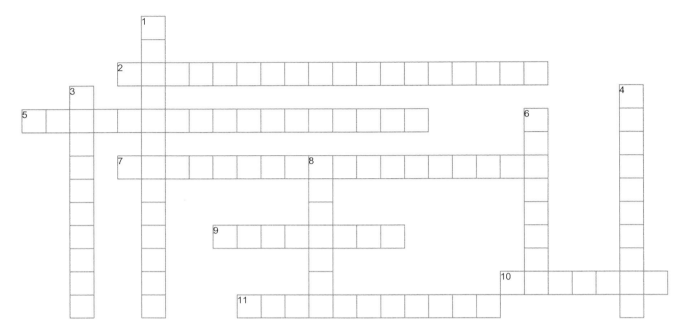

ACROSS

2. The number of red blood cells, white blood cells and platelets (per cubic millimeter) that are present in the patient's sample of blood is determined.

5. The circulatory system is composed of the heart, arteries, capillaries and veins.

7. Group of plasma protein substances (Factor I thru XIII) contained in the plasma, which act together to bring about blood coagulation.

9. Nearest to any other point of reference.

10. Having molecular oxygen present.

11. The layer of cells lining the closed internal spaces of the body such as the blood vessels and lymphatic vessels.

DOWN

1. The major human blood type system which depends on the presence or absence of antigens known as A and B.

3. The viscid, translucent fluid that makes up the essential material of all plant and animal cells.

4. The oxygen carrying pigment of the red blood cells.

6. One of the minute particles seen with the electron microscope in many types of cells, containing various hydrolytic enzymes and normally involved in the process of localized digestion inside the cell.

8. Outside the living body; inside a glass; observable in a test tube.

A. Protoplasm
D. Circulatory System
G. Coagulation factors
J. Lysosome

B. Invitro
E. Aerobic
H. Endothelium
K. ABO Blood Group

C. Hemoglobin
F. Complete blood count
I. Proximal

14. *Using the Across and Down clues, write the correct words in the numbered grid below.*

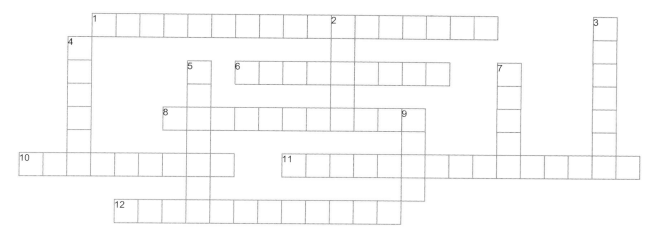

ACROSS

1. A transient vascular and neurogenic reaction marked by pallor, nausea, sweating, slowing heart rate and a rapid fall in arterial blood pressure which may result in loss of consciousness.

6. A small needle with two plastic wings attached which are squeezed together to form a tab that is used to manipulate the needle.

8. An acute, generalized life-threatening allergic or hypersensitive reaction.

10. The conversion of blood from a liquid form to solid through the process of coagulation.

11. Blood sample tubes containing a vacuum. When the tube stopper is pierced by a Vacutainer needle which has been properly positioned in a vein, the vacuum draws blood into the tube.

12. A test which measures the time it takes for small blood vessels to close off and bleeding to stop.

DOWN

2. The swelling of soft tissues caused by excess fluid accumulation.

3. To examine or feel by the hand. In relation to venipunctures, this technique is used to "feel" a vein which will tend to rebound when slight pressure is applied with the finger.

4. Inside the living body.

5. Fainting; a temporary loss of consciousness due to a reduction of blood to the brain.

7. Pertaining to the palm or sole; indicating the flexor portion of the forearm, wrist or hand.

9. Abbreviation for the Latin word statim, meaning immediately.

A. Syncope	B. Bleeding time	C. Edema	D. Vacutainer tube
E. Butterfly	F. Volar	G. Anaphylaxis	H. Palpate
I. Vasovagal response	J. Blood clot	K. Invivo	L. Stat

15. *Using the Across and Down clues, write the correct words in the numbered grid below.*

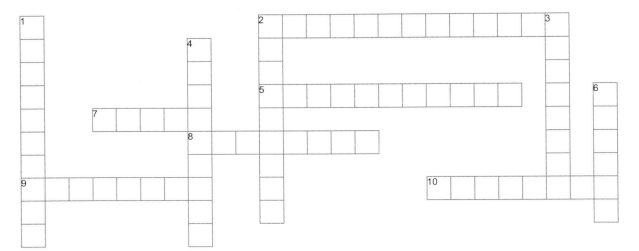

ACROSS

2. The major human blood type system which depends on the presence or absence of antigens known as A and B.

5. Cells that carry oxygen to all parts of the body.

7. Needle diameter is measured by gauge; the larger the needle diameter, the smaller the gauge.

8. A granular leukocyte with an irregularly shaped nucleus that is partially constricted into two lobes, and with cytoplasm that contains coarse, bluish-black granules of variable size.

9. Carrying away. An artery is an efferent vessel carrying blood away from the heart.

10. Pertaining to or composed of blood vessels. The vascular system is composed of the heart, blood vessels, lymphatics and their parts considered collectively.

DOWN

1. A sample of blood is applied to a microscope slide and then studied under the microscope.

2. Growing, living or occurring in the absence of molecular oxygen; pertaining to an anaerobe.

3. Nearest to any other point of reference.

4. Inflammation of a vein. The condition is marked by infiltration of the layers of the vein and the formation of a clot. It produces edema, stiffness and pain in the affected area.

6. Blood vessel carrying blood away from the heart. Arterial blood is normally full of oxygen.

A. Gauge	B. ABO Blood Group	C. Phlebitis	D. Blood smear
E. Vascular	F. Proximal	G. Efferent	H. Basophil
I. Artery	J. Anaerobic	K. Erythrocyte	

16. *Using the Across and Down clues, write the correct words in the numbered grid below.*

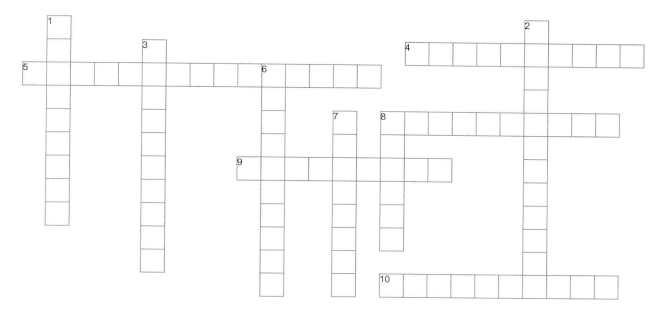

ACROSS

4. A constrictive band, placed over an extremity to distend veins for blood aspiration or intravenous injections.

5. Safety cabinets with air flow in such a direction as to carry any harmful materials or fumes away from the worker.

8. A drug that causes unconsciousness or a loss of general sensation. A local anesthetic causes loss of feeling in a part of the body.

9. The breaking of the red blood cells membrane releasing free hemoglobin into the circulating blood.

10. An organ or tissue taken from the body for grafting into another part of the same body or into another individual.

DOWN

1. The process of clot formation. Part of an important host defense mechanism call hemostasis.

2. A count made on a stained blood smear of the proportion of the different leukocytes (WBC's) and expressed as a percentage.

3. Any of the many forms of mononuclear phagocytes found in tissues and originating from stem cells in the bone marrow. In normal circulation, the monocyte may be categorized as a macrophage.

6. Blood from which none of the elements have been removed.

7. An antigenic substance capable of producing an immediate-type hypersensitivity (allergy).

8. To attract and retain other material on the surface.

A. Laminar flow hood
E. Hemolysis
I. Anesthetic

B. Adsorb
F. Coagulate
J. Differential

C. Whole blood
G. Allergen
K. Tourniquet

D. Macrophage
H. Transplant

17. *Using the Across and Down clues, write the correct words in the numbered grid below.*

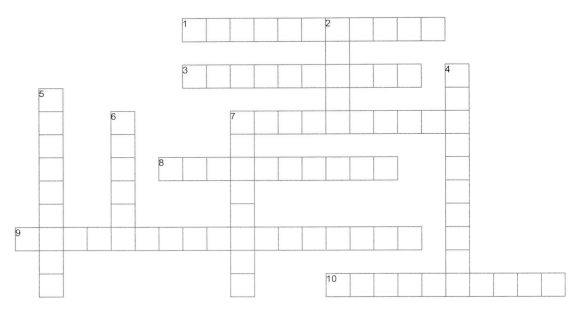

ACROSS

1. Terminology used to define the order in which blood sample tubes should be drawn using a multi-sample technique such as the Vacutainer System.

3. Infectious. May be transmitted from person to person.

7. The most common form of hepatitis after blood transfusion. It is also the most prevalent form resulting from needle sharing by drug abusers.

8. A type of swelling which occurs in lymphatic tissue when excess fluid collects in the arms or legs because the lymph nodes or vessels are blocked or removed.

9. A state in which the body reacts with an exaggerated immune response to a foreign substance. Reactions are classified as delayed or immediate types.

10. The outside layer of cells that covers all the free, open surfaces of the body including the skin, and mucous membranes that communicate with the outside of the body.

DOWN

2. A sudden loss of consciousness.

4. Any of the many forms of mononuclear phagocytes found in tissues and originating from stem cells in the bone marrow. In normal circulation, the monocyte may be categorized as a macrophage.

5. White blood cells.

6. Referring to the palm surface or side of the hand

7. An anticoagulant that acts to inhibit coagulation factors, especially factor Xa. Heparin is formed in the liver.

A. Palmar B. Leukocyte C. Lymphedema D. Contagious
E. Heparin F. Hypersensitivity G. Epithelium H. Macrophage
I. Order of Draw J. Hepatitis C K. Faint

18. *Using the Across and Down clues, write the correct words in the numbered grid below.*

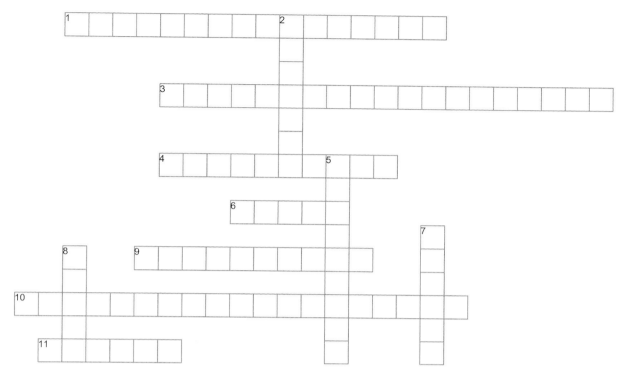

ACROSS

1. The selective separation and removal of platelets from withdrawn blood. The remainder of the blood is re-transfused back into the donor.

3. A hospital-borne infection. An infection whose origin is from within the hospital environment.

4. The oxygen carrying pigment of the red blood cells.

6. A glass or transparent plastic tube used to accurately measure small amounts of liquid.

9. A trade name now a generic term used to describe equipment used to automatically aspirate blood from a vessel by venipuncture.

10. Any different protein factors which, when acting together, can form a blood clot shortly after platelets have broken at the site of the wound.

11. A very tiny vein, continuous with the capillaries. Compare with arteriole.

DOWN

2. Pertaining to elements dissolved in blood or body fluids, e.g., homoral immunity from antibodies in the blood as opposed to cellular immunity.

5. A small needle with two plastic wings attached which are squeezed together to form a tab that is used to manipulate the needle.

7. To attract and retain other material on the surface.

8. Lying face down; opposed to supine.

A. Adsorb
D. Nosocomial infection
G. Butterfly
J. Venule

B. Plateletpheresis
E. Prone
H. Hemoglobin
K. Humoral

C. Vacutainer
F. Blood clotting factor
I. Pipet

19. *Using the Across and Down clues, write the correct words in the numbered grid below.*

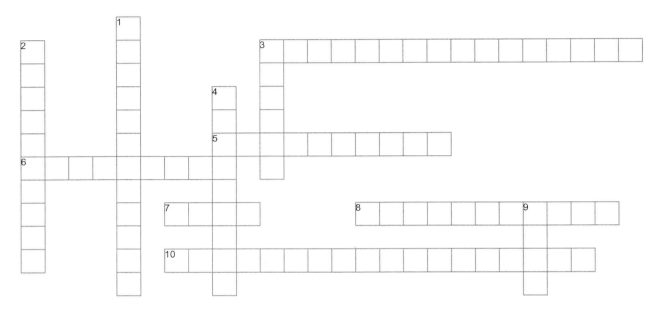

ACROSS

3. A method used by microbiologists and clinicians to keep cultures, sterile instruments and media, and people free of microbial contamination.

5. The formation of a blood clot (thrombus) within a vessel.

6. The process of clot formation. Part of an important host defense mechanism call hemostasis.

7. Blood vessels carrying blood to the heart. Blood contained within these vessels is generally bound with carbon dioxide which will be exchanged for oxygen in the lungs.

8. Formation of profuse perspiration (sweat). A symptom of syncope or vasovagal response.

10. A device used with a butterfly and Vacutainer holder to allow for the withdrawal of multiple tubes of blood during a venipuncture

DOWN

1. A test which involves the incubation of a blood specimen overnight to determine if bacteria are present.

2. The determination of the proper number of red blood cells, white blood cells and platelets are present in the patient's blood.

3. Blood vessel carrying blood away from the heart. Arterial blood is normally full of oxygen.

4. A small branch of an artery that leads to a capillary. Also, see capillary.

9. A calcium chelating (binding) agent that is used as an anticoagulant for laboratory blood specimens. Also used in treatment of lead poisoning.

A. Diaphoretic   B. Multi sample adapter   C. Arteriole   D. Artery
E. Coagulate   F. Blood count   G. Aseptic technique   H. Thrombosis
I. Vein   J. EDTA   K. Blood culture

20. *Using the Across and Down clues, write the correct words in the numbered grid below.*

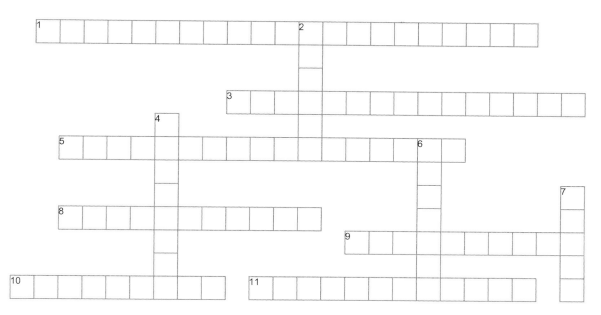

ACROSS

1. Blood which infuses an area through a secondary or accessory route.

3. Blood obtained from the circulation away from the heart, such as from the fingertip, heel pad, earlobe or from an antecubital vein.

5. Hemoglobin which has been bound with carbon monoxide, which has an affinity for hemoglobin 200 times greater than oxygen.

8. Pertaining to results obtained through treatment; having medicinal or healing properties; a healing agent.

9. The viscid, translucent fluid that makes up the essential material of all plant and animal cells.

10. An outflow, usually of fluid.

11. The science concerned with the study of factors influencing the distribution of disease and their causes in a defined population.

DOWN

2. Inside the living body.

4. A brand name for warfarin sodium.

6. Outside the living body; inside a glass; observable in a test tube.

7. Fluid found in lymphatic vessels and nodes derived from tissue fluids. Lymph is collected from all parts of the body and returned to the blood by the lymphatic system.

A. Effluent
B. Epidemiology
C. Therapeutic
D. Peripheral blood
E. Invitro
F. Invivo
G. Collateral circulation
H. Carboxyhemoglobin
I. Lymph
J. Coumadin
K. Protoplasm

1. *Using the Across and Down clues, write the correct words in the numbered grid below.*

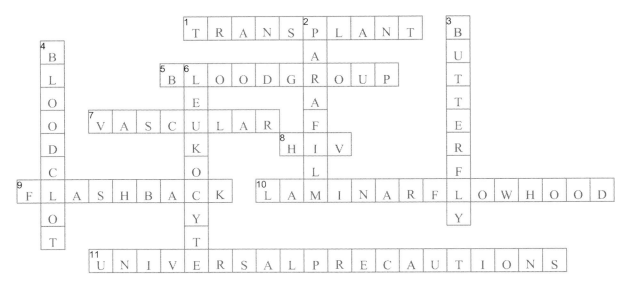

ACROSS

1. An organ or tissue taken from the body for grafting into another part of the same body or into another individual.

5. An inherited feature on the surface of the red blood cell. A series of related blood groups make up a blood group system such as the ABO system or the Rh system.

7. Pertaining to or composed of blood vessels. The vascular system is composed of the heart, blood vessels, lymphatics and their parts considered collectively.

8. Human Immunodeficiency Virus

9. Relative to venipunctures, the appearance of a small amount of blood in the neck of a syringe or the tubing of a butterfly. This is a sign that the vein has been properly accessed.

10. Safety cabinets with air flow in such a direction as to carry any harmful materials or fumes away from the worker.

11. A set of procedures and protocols designed to protect the healthcare worker which uses the basic concept that each patient must be treated as though they were infected with an infectious disease.

DOWN

2. A thin film of paraffin used primarily in the laboratory to seal open containers such as test tubes.

3. A small needle with two plastic wings attached which are squeezed together to form a tab that is used to manipulate the needle.

4. The conversion of blood from a liquid form to solid through the process of coagulation.

6. White blood cells.

A. Vascular
D. Universal Precautions
G. Parafilm
J. Leukocyte

B. HIV
E. Butterfly
H. Blood group
K. Flash back

C. Blood clot
F. Laminar flow hood
I. Transplant

2. Using the Across and Down clues, write the correct words in the numbered grid below.

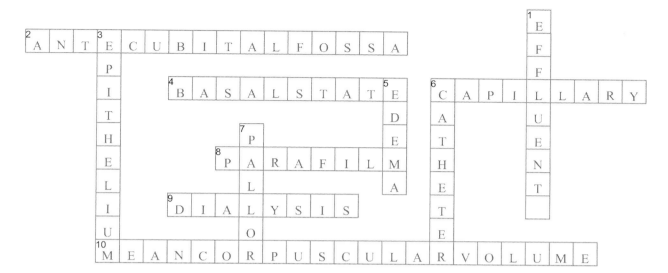

ACROSS

2. That part of the arm opposing the elbow.

4. The state of the body early in the morning, approximately 12 hours after the last ingestion of food or other nutrition.

6. Any one of the minute vessels that connect the arterioles and venules, forming a network in nearly all parts of the body.

8. A thin film of paraffin used primarily in the laboratory to seal open containers such as test tubes.

9. The process of cleansing the blood by passing it through a special machine. Dialysis is necessary when the kidneys are not able to filter the blood.

10. Average volume of red blood cells.

DOWN

1. An outflow, usually of fluid.

3. The outside layer of cells that covers all the free, open surfaces of the body including the skin, and mucous membranes that communicate with the outside of the body.

5. The swelling of soft tissues caused by excess fluid accumulation.

6. A thin, flexible tube. When a catheter is placed in a vein, it provides a pathway for giving drugs, nutrients, fluids, or blood products.

7. Paleness; decrease of absence of skin color.

A. Capillary
D. Dialysis
G. Epithelium
J. Basal state

B. Antecubital fossa
E. Parafilm
H. Pallor
K. Effluent

C. Catheter
F. Edema
I. Mean Corpuscular Volume

3. *Using the Across and Down clues, write the correct words in the numbered grid below.*

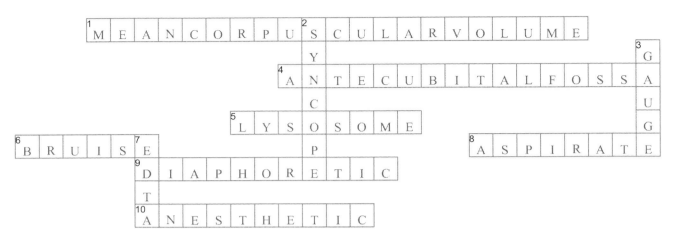

ACROSS

1. Average volume of red blood cells.

4. That part of the arm opposing the elbow.

5. One of the minute particles seen with the electron microscope in many types of cells, containing various hydrolytic enzymes and normally involved in the process of localized digestion inside the cell.

6. A bruise or ""contusion" is a traumatic injury of the soft tissues which results in breakage of the local capillaries and leakage of red blood cells.

8. As it relates to blood drawing, the material that is withdrawn with a negative pressure apparatus (syringe).

9. Formation of profuse perspiration (sweat). A symptom of syncope or vasovagal response.

10. A drug that causes unconsciousness or a loss of general sensation. A local anesthetic causes loss of feeling in a part of the body.

DOWN

2. Fainting; a temporary loss of consciousness due to a reduction of blood to the brain.

3. Needle diameter is measured by gauge; the larger the needle diameter, the smaller the gauge.

7. A calcium chelating (binding) agent that is used as an anticoagulant for laboratory blood specimens. Also used in treatment of lead poisoning.

A. Gauge
D. Antecubital fossa
G. Lysosome
J. Syncope

B. EDTA
E. Mean Corpuscular Volume
H. Anesthetic

C. Aspirate
F. Bruise
I. Diaphoretic

4. *Using the Across and Down clues, write the correct words in the numbered grid below.*

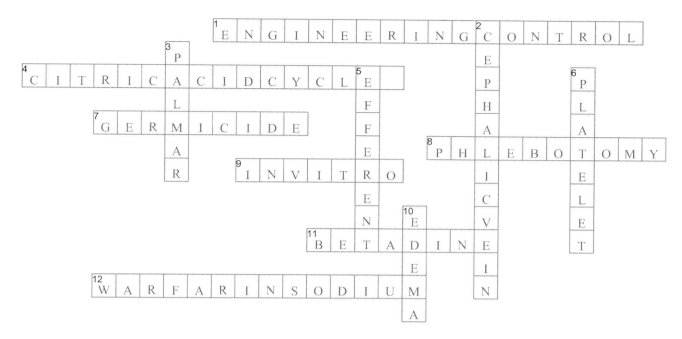

ACROSS

1. Controls (e.g., sharps disposal containers, self-sheathing needles) that isolate or remove the bloodborne pathogens hazard from the workplace.

4. A group or series of enzymatic reactions in living aerobic organisms that results in the production of energy.

7. An agent that kills pathogenic microorganisms

8. The incision of a vein as for blood-letting (venesection); needle puncture of a vein for drawing blood (venipuncture).

9. Outside the living body; inside a glass; observable in a test tube.

11. A popular tradename iodine-containing topical antiseptic agent; povidone-iodine.

12. The sodium salt of warfarin, one of the synthetic anticoagulants. Coumadin is a brand name.

DOWN

2. A large vein of the arm that empties into the axillary vein

3. Referring to the palm surface or side of the hand

5. Carrying away. An artery is an efferent vessel carrying blood away from the heart.

6. Also known as a thrombocyte, this is a particulate component of the blood known for its involvement in blood coagulation.

10. The swelling of soft tissues caused by excess fluid accumulation.

A. Citric Acid Cycle	B. Betadine	C. Edema	D. Warfarin sodium
E. Phlebotomy	F. Platelet	G. Invitro	H. Engineering control
I. Efferent	J. Cephalic vein	K. Germicide	L. Palmar

5. *Using the Across and Down clues, write the correct words in the numbered grid below.*

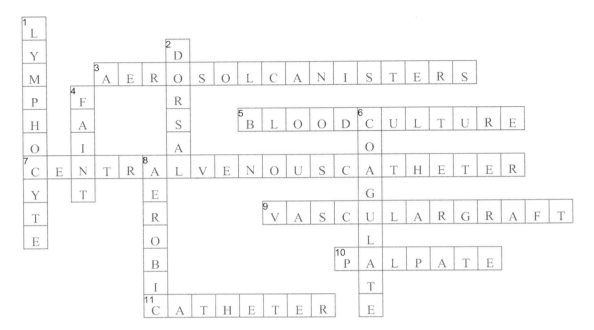

ACROSS

3. Enclosed containers used to hold specimen tubes for centrifugation.

5. A test which involves the incubation of a blood specimen overnight to determine if bacteria are present.

7. Small, flexible plastic tube inserted into the large vein above the heart, through which drugs and blood products can be given and blood samples withdrawn painlessly.

9. A type of an arteriovenous fistula consisting of either a venous autograft or synthetic tube which is grafted to the artery and vein.

10. To examine or feel by the hand. In relation to venipunctures, this technique is used to "feel" a vein which will tend to rebound when slight pressure is applied with the finger.

11. A thin, flexible tube. When a catheter is placed in a vein, it provides a pathway for giving drugs, nutrients, fluids, or blood products.

DOWN

1. Any of the mononuclear, nonphagocytic leukocytes, found in the blood and lymph, which are the body's immunologically competent cells.

2. Denoting a position more toward the back surface than some other object of reference; same as posterior in human anatomy.

4. A sudden loss of consciousness.

6. The process of clot formation. Part of an important host defense mechanism call hemostasis.

8. Having molecular oxygen present.

A. Aerobic
D. Palpate
G. Vascular graft
J. Catheter

B. Coagulate
E. Blood culture
H. Faint
K. Central venous catheter

C. Lymphocyte
F. Dorsal
I. Aerosol canisters

6. *Using the Across and Down clues, write the correct words in the numbered grid below.*

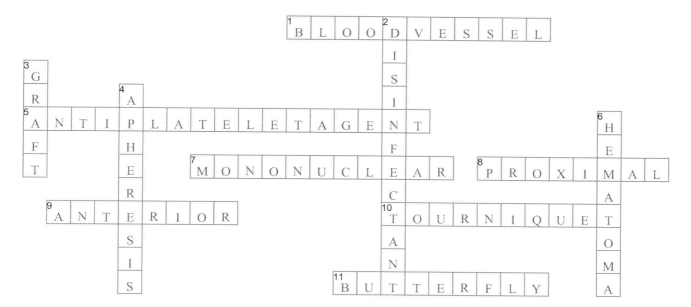

ACROSS

1. All the vessels lined with endothelium through which blood circulates.

5. Medications that, like aspirin, reduce the tendency of platelets in the blood to clump and clot.

7. A cell containing but one nucleus. In blood circulation, monocyte and lymphocyte.

8. Nearest to any other point of reference.

9. Toward the front or in front of.

10. A constrictive band, placed over an extremity to distend veins for blood aspiration or intravenous injections.

11. A small needle with two plastic wings attached which are squeezed together to form a tab that is used to manipulate the needle.

DOWN

2. An agent that disinfects, applied particularly to agents used on inanimate objects.

3. An implant or transplant of any tissue or organ.

4. A technique in which blood products are separated from a donor and the desired elements collected and the rest returned to the donor.

6. A localized collection of blood within tissue due to leakage from the wall of a blood vessel, producing a bluish discoloration (ecchymosis)and pain.

A. Disinfectant   B. Tourniquet   C. Antiplatelet agent   D. Hematoma
E. Butterfly   F. Apheresis   G. Graft   H. Blood vessel
I. Mononuclear   J. Proximal   K. Anterior

7. *Using the Across and Down clues, write the correct words in the numbered grid below.*

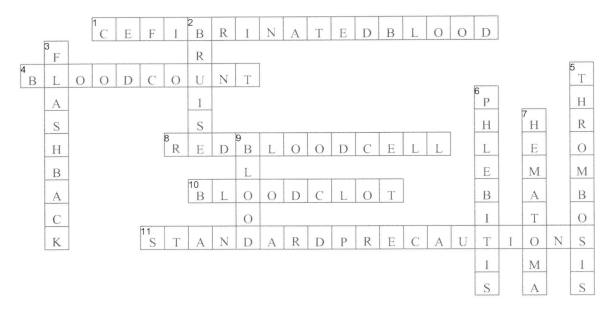

ACROSS

1. Blood which has been deprived of fibrin.

4. The determination of the proper number of red blood cells, white blood cells and platelets are present in the patient's blood.

8. The component of the blood that contains hemoglobin which is responsible for oxygen and carbon dioxide exchange.

10. The conversion of blood from a liquid form to solid through the process of coagulation.

11. Precautions that are designed for the care of all patients in hospitals regardless of their diagnosis or presumed infection status.

DOWN

2. A bruise or ""contusion" is a traumatic injury of the soft tissues which results in breakage of the local capillaries and leakage of red blood cells.

3. Relative to venipunctures, the appearance of a small amount of blood in the neck of a syringe or the tubing of a butterfly. This is a sign that the vein has been properly accessed.

5. The formation of a blood clot (thrombus) within a vessel.

6. Inflammation of a vein. The condition is marked by infiltration of the layers of the vein and the formation of a clot. It produces edema, stiffness and pain in the affected area.

7. A localized collection of blood within tissue due to leakage from the wall of a blood vessel, producing a bluish discoloration (ecchymosis)and pain.

9. The fluid in the body that contains red cells and white cells as well as platelets, proteins, plasma and other elements. It is transported throughout the body by the Circulatory System.

A. Phlebitis
E. Blood count
I. Hematoma

B. Blood clot
F. Thrombosis
J. Standard Precautions

C. Bruise
G. Blood
K. Cefibrinated blood

D. Flash back
H. Red blood cell

8. *Using the Across and Down clues, write the correct words in the numbered grid below.*

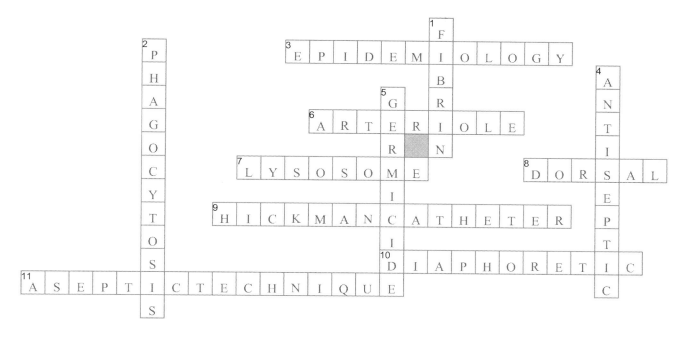

ACROSS

3. The science concerned with the study of factors influencing the distribution of disease and their causes in a defined population.

6. A small branch of an artery that leads to a capillary. Also, see capillary.

7. One of the minute particles seen with the electron microscope in many types of cells, containing various hydrolytic enzymes and normally involved in the process of localized digestion inside the cell.

8. Denoting a position more toward the back surface than some other object of reference; same as posterior in human anatomy.

9. A hollow silicone (soft, rubber-like material) tube inserted and secured into a large vein in the chest for long-term use to administer drugs or nutrients.

10. Formation of profuse perspiration (sweat). A symptom of syncope or vasovagal response.

11. A method used by microbiologists and clinicians to keep cultures, sterile instruments and media, and people free of microbial contamination.

DOWN

1. The protein formed during normal blood clotting that is the essence of the clot.

2. A process where polymorphonuclear leukocytes, monocytes, and macrophages combine with lysosomes within the cell cytoplasm to digest and destroy a particulate.

4. Something that discourages the growth microorganisms. By contrast, aseptic refers to the absence of microorganisms.

5. An agent that kills pathogenic microorganisms

A. Arteriole
E. Lysosome
I. Fibrin

B. Epidemiology
F. Dorsal
J. Aseptic technique

C. Diaphoretic
G. Hickman catheter
K. Phagocytosis

D. Germicide
H. Antiseptic

9. *Using the Across and Down clues, write the correct words in the numbered grid below.*

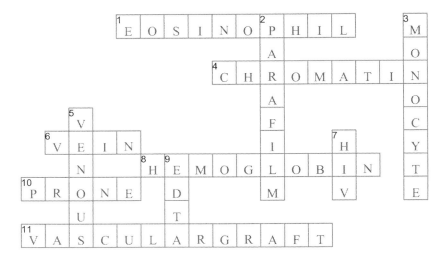

ACROSS

1. An eosin (red) staining leukocyte with a nucleus that usually has two lobes connected by a slender thread of chromatin, and cytoplasm containing coarse, round granules that are uniform in size.

4. The more readily stainable portion of the cell nucleus. It is a DNA attached to a protein structure and is the carrier of genes in inheritance.

6. Blood vessels carrying blood to the heart. Blood contained within these vessels is generally bound with carbon dioxide which will be exchanged for oxygen in the lungs.

8. The oxygen carrying pigment of the red blood cells.

10. Lying face down; opposed to supine.

11. A type of an arteriovenous fistula consisting of either a venous autograft or synthetic tube which is grafted to the artery and vein.

DOWN

2. A thin film of paraffin used primarily in the laboratory to seal open containers such as test tubes.

3. A mononuclear, phagocytic leukocyte.

5. Pertaining to the veins, or blood passing through them.

7. Human Immunodeficiency Virus

9. A calcium chelating (binding) agent that is used as an anticoagulant for laboratory blood specimens. Also used in treatment of lead poisoning.

A. Eosinophil   B. Vascular graft   C. Vein   D. Chromatin   E. Venous
F. Prone   G. HIV   H. Monocyte   I. EDTA   J. Hemoglobin
K. Parafilm

10. *Using the Across and Down clues, write the correct words in the numbered grid below.*

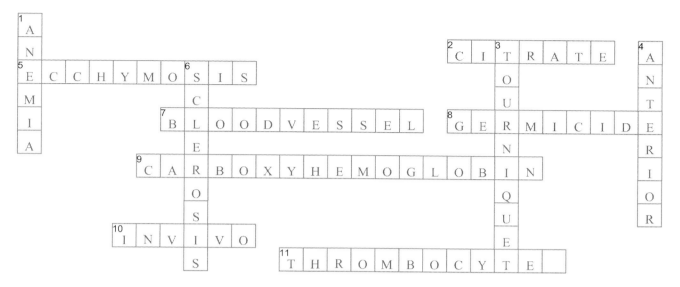

ACROSS

2. A compound that is an intermediate in the citric acid cycle (Krebs cycle or glycolysis). Citrate chelates (binds) calcium ions, preventing blood clotting and, thus, is an effective anticoagulant.

5. The skin discoloration caused by a bruise (contusion).

7. All the vessels lined with endothelium through which blood circulates.

8. An agent that kills pathogenic microorganisms

9. Hemoglobin which has been bound with carbon monoxide, which has an affinity for hemoglobin 200 times greater than oxygen.

10. Inside the living body.

11. Also known as a platelet, this is a particulate component of the blood, approximately 2-4 microns in diameter and known for its involvement in blood coagulation.

DOWN

1. The condition of having less than the normal number of red blood cells or hemoglobin in the blood.

3. A constrictive band, placed over an extremity to distend veins for blood aspiration or intravenous injections.

4. Toward the front or in front of.

6. A hardening, especially from inflammation and certain disease states. Though sclerosis may occur in many areas of the body, the term is most often associated with blood vessels.

A. Invivo
E. Ecchymosis
I. Tourniquet

B. Anterior
F. Sclerosis
J. Thrombocyte

C. Blood vessel
G. Carboxyhemoglobin
K. Citrate

D. Germicide
H. Anemia

11. *Using the Across and Down clues, write the correct words in the numbered grid below.*

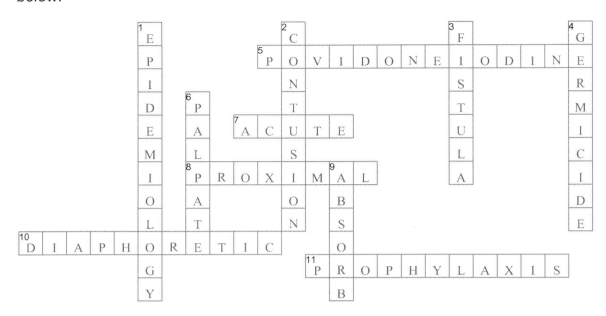

ACROSS

5. Used as a topical antiseptic, this is a compound made by reacting iodine with povidone which slowly releases iodine.

7. Of short duration. Rapid and abbreviated in onset.

8. Nearest to any other point of reference.

10. Formation of profuse perspiration (sweat). A symptom of syncope or vasovagal response.

11. A preventative treatment.

DOWN

1. The science concerned with the study of factors influencing the distribution of disease and their causes in a defined population.

2. A bruise or injury without a break in the skin.

3. An abnormal passageway usually between two internal organs. Such passages may be created experimentally for obtaining body secretions for study.

4. An agent that kills pathogenic microorganisms

6. To examine or feel by the hand. In relation to venipunctures, this technique is used to "feel" a vein which will tend to rebound when slight pressure is applied with the finger.

9. To suck up, as through pores.

A. Palpate
E. Povidone iodine
I. Diaphoretic

B. Proximal
F. Prophylaxis
J. Absorb

C. Germicide
G. Acute
K. Epidemiology

D. Fistula
H. Contusion

12. *Using the Across and Down clues, write the correct words in the numbered grid below.*

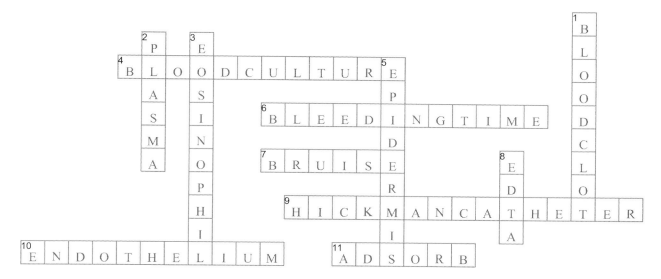

ACROSS

4. A test which involves the incubation of a blood specimen overnight to determine if bacteria are present.

6. A test which measures the time it takes for small blood vessels to close off and bleeding to stop.

7. A bruise or ""contusion" is a traumatic injury of the soft tissues which results in breakage of the local capillaries and leakage of red blood cells.

9. A hollow silicone (soft, rubber-like material) tube inserted and secured into a large vein in the chest for long-term use to administer drugs or nutrients.

10. The layer of cells lining the closed internal spaces of the body such as the blood vessels and lymphatic vessels.

11. To attract and retain other material on the surface.

DOWN

1. The conversion of blood from a liquid form to solid through the process of coagulation.

2. The fluid portion of the blood in which the cellular components are suspended. Plasma contains coagulation factors used in the clotting of blood as opposed to serum.

3. An eosin (red) staining leukocyte with a nucleus that usually has two lobes connected by a slender thread of chromatin, and cytoplasm containing coarse, round granules that are uniform in size.

5. The upper or outer layer of the two main layers of cells that make up the skin.

8. A calcium chelating (binding) agent that is used as an anticoagulant for laboratory blood specimens. Also used in treatment of lead poisoning.

A. Epidermis
E. Adsorb
I. Bruise

B. Plasma
F. Hickman catheter
J. Blood culture

C. Bleeding time
G. Eosinophil
K. Endothelium

D. Blood clot
H. EDTA

13. *Using the Across and Down clues, write the correct words in the numbered grid below.*

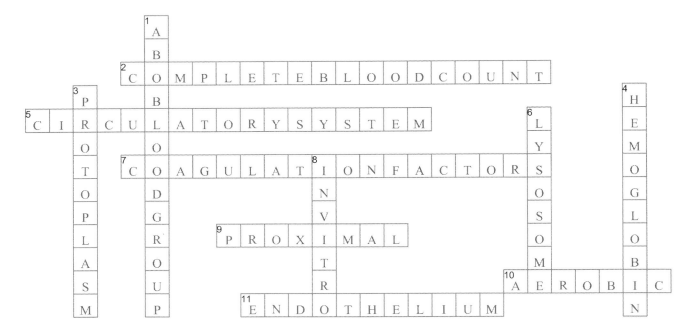

ACROSS

2. The number of red blood cells, white blood cells and platelets (per cubic millimeter) that are present in the patient's sample of blood is determined.

5. The circulatory system is composed of the heart, arteries, capillaries and veins.

7. Group of plasma protein substances (Factor I thru XIII) contained in the plasma, which act together to bring about blood coagulation.

9. Nearest to any other point of reference.

10. Having molecular oxygen present.

11. The layer of cells lining the closed internal spaces of the body such as the blood vessels and lymphatic vessels.

DOWN

1. The major human blood type system which depends on the presence or absence of antigens known as A and B.

3. The viscid, translucent fluid that makes up the essential material of all plant and animal cells.

4. The oxygen carrying pigment of the red blood cells.

6. One of the minute particles seen with the electron microscope in many types of cells, containing various hydrolytic enzymes and normally involved in the process of localized digestion inside the cell.

8. Outside the living body; inside a glass; observable in a test tube.

A. Protoplasm
D. Circulatory System
G. Coagulation factors
J. Lysosome

B. Invitro
E. Aerobic
H. Endothelium
K. ABO Blood Group

C. Hemoglobin
F. Complete blood count
I. Proximal

14. *Using the Across and Down clues, write the correct words in the numbered grid below.*

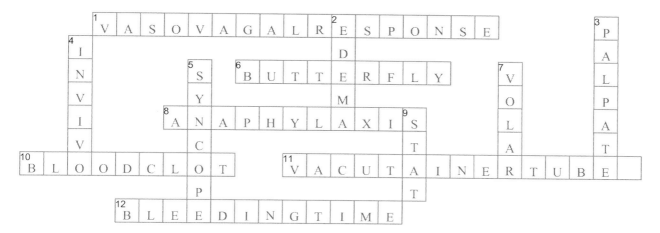

ACROSS

1. A transient vascular and neurogenic reaction marked by pallor, nausea, sweating, slowing heart rate and a rapid fall in arterial blood pressure which may result in loss of consciousness.

6. A small needle with two plastic wings attached which are squeezed together to form a tab that is used to manipulate the needle.

8. An acute, generalized life-threatening allergic or hypersensitive reaction.

10. The conversion of blood from a liquid form to solid through the process of coagulation.

11. Blood sample tubes containing a vacuum. When the tube stopper is pierced by a Vacutainer needle which has been properly positioned in a vein, the vacuum draws blood into the tube.

12. A test which measures the time it takes for small blood vessels to close off and bleeding to stop.

DOWN

2. The swelling of soft tissues caused by excess fluid accumulation.

3. To examine or feel by the hand. In relation to venipunctures, this technique is used to "feel" a vein which will tend to rebound when slight pressure is applied with the finger.

4. Inside the living body.

5. Fainting; a temporary loss of consciousness due to a reduction of blood to the brain.

7. Pertaining to the palm or sole; indicating the flexor portion of the forearm, wrist or hand.

9. Abbreviation for the Latin word statim, meaning immediately.

A. Syncope
E. Butterfly
I. Vasovagal response

B. Bleeding time
F. Volar
J. Blood clot

C. Edema
G. Anaphylaxis
K. Invivo

D. Vacutainer tube
H. Palpate
L. Stat

15. *Using the Across and Down clues, write the correct words in the numbered grid below.*

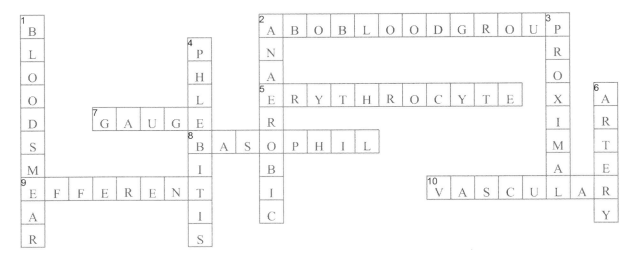

ACROSS

2. The major human blood type system which depends on the presence or absence of antigens known as A and B.

5. Cells that carry oxygen to all parts of the body.

7. Needle diameter is measured by gauge; the larger the needle diameter, the smaller the gauge.

8. A granular leukocyte with an irregularly shaped nucleus that is partially constricted into two lobes, and with cytoplasm that contains coarse, bluish-black granules of variable size.

9. Carrying away. An artery is an efferent vessel carrying blood away from the heart.

10. Pertaining to or composed of blood vessels. The vascular system is composed of the heart, blood vessels, lymphatics and their parts considered collectively.

DOWN

1. A sample of blood is applied to a microscope slide and then studied under the microscope.

2. Growing, living or occurring in the absence of molecular oxygen; pertaining to an anaerobe.

3. Nearest to any other point of reference.

4. Inflammation of a vein. The condition is marked by infiltration of the layers of the vein and the formation of a clot. It produces edema, stiffness and pain in the affected area.

6. Blood vessel carrying blood away from the heart. Arterial blood is normally full of oxygen.

A. Gauge	B. ABO Blood Group	C. Phlebitis	D. Blood smear
E. Vascular	F. Proximal	G. Efferent	H. Basophil
I. Artery	J. Anaerobic	K. Erythrocyte	

16. *Using the Across and Down clues, write the correct words in the numbered grid below.*

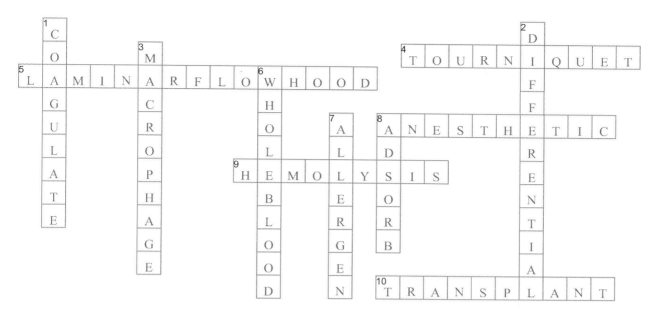

ACROSS

4. A constrictive band, placed over an extremity to distend veins for blood aspiration or intravenous injections.

5. Safety cabinets with air flow in such a direction as to carry any harmful materials or fumes away from the worker.

8. A drug that causes unconsciousness or a loss of general sensation. A local anesthetic causes loss of feeling in a part of the body.

9. The breaking of the red blood cells membrane releasing free hemoglobin into the circulating blood.

10. An organ or tissue taken from the body for grafting into another part of the same body or into another individual.

DOWN

1. The process of clot formation. Part of an important host defense mechanism call hemostasis.

2. A count made on a stained blood smear of the proportion of the different leukocytes (WBC's) and expressed as a percentage.

3. Any of the many forms of mononuclear phagocytes found in tissues and originating from stem cells in the bone marrow. In normal circulation, the monocyte may be categorized as a macrophage.

6. Blood from which none of the elements have been removed.

7. An antigenic substance capable of producing an immediate-type hypersensitivity (allergy).

8. To attract and retain other material on the surface.

A. Laminar flow hood
B. Adsorb
C. Whole blood
D. Macrophage
E. Hemolysis
F. Coagulate
G. Allergen
H. Transplant
I. Anesthetic
J. Differential
K. Tourniquet

17. *Using the Across and Down clues, write the correct words in the numbered grid below.*

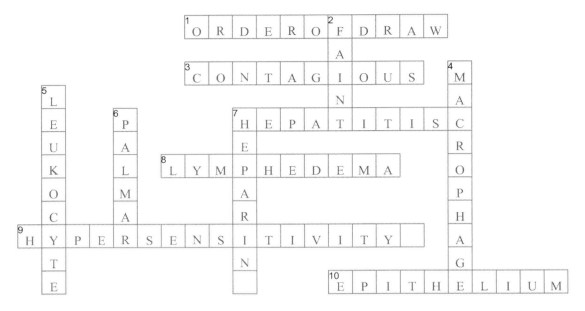

ACROSS

1. Terminology used to define the order in which blood sample tubes should be drawn using a multi-sample technique such as the Vacutainer System.

3. Infectious. May be transmitted from person to person.

7. The most common form of hepatitis after blood transfusion. It is also the most prevalent form resulting from needle sharing by drug abusers.

8. A type of swelling which occurs in lymphatic tissue when excess fluid collects in the arms or legs because the lymph nodes or vessels are blocked or removed.

9. A state in which the body reacts with an exaggerated immune response to a foreign substance. Reactions are classified as delayed or immediate types.

10. The outside layer of cells that covers all the free, open surfaces of the body including the skin, and mucous membranes that communicate with the outside of the body.

DOWN

2. A sudden loss of consciousness.

4. Any of the many forms of mononuclear phagocytes found in tissues and originating from stem cells in the bone marrow. In normal circulation, the monocyte may be categorized as a macrophage.

5. White blood cells.

6. Referring to the palm surface or side of the hand

7. An anticoagulant that acts to inhibit coagulation factors, especially factor Xa. Heparin is formed in the liver.

A. Palmar
E. Heparin
I. Order of Draw
B. Leukocyte
F. Hypersensitivity
J. Hepatitis C
C. Lymphedema
G. Epithelium
K. Faint
D. Contagious
H. Macrophage

18. *Using the Across and Down clues, write the correct words in the numbered grid below.*

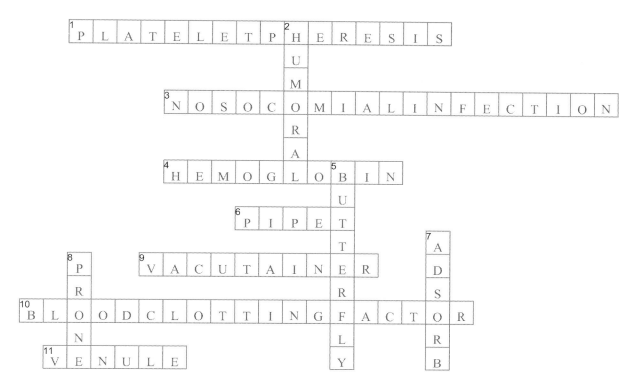

ACROSS

1. The selective separation and removal of platelets from withdrawn blood. The remainder of the blood is re-transfused back into the donor.

3. A hospital-borne infection. An infection whose origin is from within the hospital environment.

4. The oxygen carrying pigment of the red blood cells.

6. A glass or transparent plastic tube used to accurately measure small amounts of liquid.

9. A trade name now a generic term used to describe equipment used to automatically aspirate blood from a vessel by venipuncture.

10. Any different protein factors which, when acting together, can form a blood clot shortly after platelets have broken at the site of the wound.

11. A very tiny vein, continuous with the capillaries. Compare with arteriole.

DOWN

2. Pertaining to elements dissolved in blood or body fluids, e.g., homoral immunity from antibodies in the blood as opposed to cellular immunity.

5. A small needle with two plastic wings attached which are squeezed together to form a tab that is used to manipulate the needle.

7. To attract and retain other material on the surface.

8. Lying face down; opposed to supine.

A. Adsorb
D. Nosocomial infection
G. Butterfly
J. Venule

B. Plateletpheresis
E. Prone
H. Hemoglobin
K. Humoral

C. Vacutainer
F. Blood clotting factor
I. Pipet

19. *Using the Across and Down clues, write the correct words in the numbered grid below.*

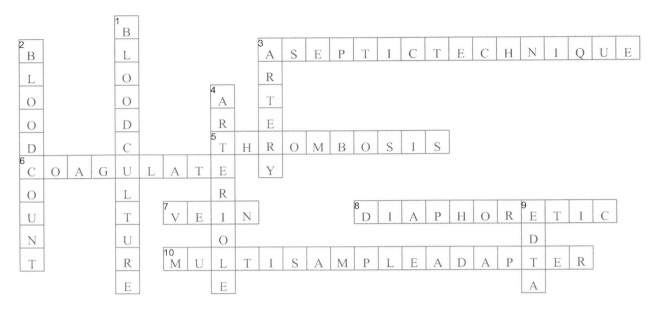

ACROSS

3. A method used by microbiologists and clinicians to keep cultures, sterile instruments and media, and people free of microbial contamination.

5. The formation of a blood clot (thrombus) within a vessel.

6. The process of clot formation. Part of an important host defense mechanism call hemostasis.

7. Blood vessels carrying blood to the heart. Blood contained within these vessels is generally bound with carbon dioxide which will be exchanged for oxygen in the lungs.

8. Formation of profuse perspiration (sweat). A symptom of syncope or vasovagal response.

10. A device used with a butterfly and Vacutainer holder to allow for the withdrawal of multiple tubes of blood during a venipuncture

DOWN

1. A test which involves the incubation of a blood specimen overnight to determine if bacteria are present.

2. The determination of the proper number of red blood cells, white blood cells and platelets are present in the patient's blood.

3. Blood vessel carrying blood away from the heart. Arterial blood is normally full of oxygen.

4. A small branch of an artery that leads to a capillary. Also, see capillary.

9. A calcium chelating (binding) agent that is used as an anticoagulant for laboratory blood specimens. Also used in treatment of lead poisoning.

A. Diaphoretic
E. Coagulate
I. Vein

B. Multi sample adapter
F. Blood count
J. EDTA

C. Arteriole
G. Aseptic technique
K. Blood culture

D. Artery
H. Thrombosis

20. *Using the Across and Down clues, write the correct words in the numbered grid below.*

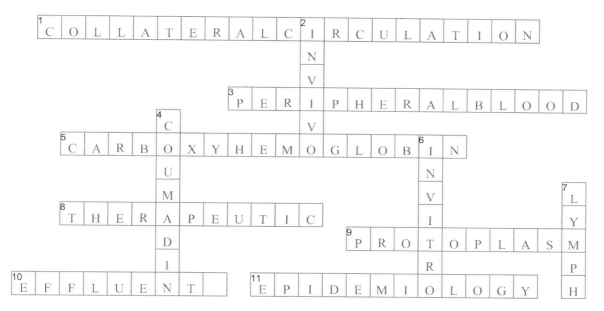

ACROSS

1. Blood which infuses an area through a secondary or accessory route.

3. Blood obtained from the circulation away from the heart, such as from the fingertip, heel pad, earlobe or from an antecubital vein.

5. Hemoglobin which has been bound with carbon monoxide, which has an affinity for hemoglobin 200 times greater than oxygen.

8. Pertaining to results obtained through treatment; having medicinal or healing properties; a healing agent.

9. The viscid, translucent fluid that makes up the essential material of all plant and animal cells.

10. An outflow, usually of fluid.

11. The science concerned with the study of factors influencing the distribution of disease and their causes in a defined population.

DOWN

2. Inside the living body.

4. A brand name for warfarin sodium.

6. Outside the living body; inside a glass; observable in a test tube.

7. Fluid found in lymphatic vessels and nodes derived from tissue fluids. Lymph is collected from all parts of the body and returned to the blood by the lymphatic system.

A. Effluent
E. Invitro
I. Lymph

B. Epidemiology
F. Invivo
J. Coumadin

C. Therapeutic
G. Collateral circulation
K. Protoplasm

D. Peripheral blood
H. Carboxyhemoglobin

Multiple Choice

From the words provided for each clue, provide the letter of the word which best matches the clue.

1. ____ A localized collection of blood within tissue due to leakage from the wall of a blood vessel, producing a bluish discoloration (ecchymosis)and pain.
A.aseptic technique   B.povidone iodine   C.adsorb   D.hematoma

2. ____ As it relates to blood drawing, the material that is withdrawn with a negative pressure apparatus (syringe).
A.hypersensitivity   B.aseptic technique   C.anticoagulant   D.aspirate

3. ____ Referring to blood, the clear liquid portion of blood that separates out after clotting has taken place. Since clotting has occurred, serum is fibrinogen deficient. Contrast to plasma.
A.transmission based precautions   B.hypersensitivity   C.serum   D.anaphylaxis

4. ____ The swelling of soft tissues caused by excess fluid accumulation.
A.germicide   B.edema   C.basal state   D.nosocomial infection

5. ____ Performing a venipuncture with no apparently visible or palpable vein.
A.vascular graft   B.blind stick   C.erythrocyte   D.whole blood

6. ____ An anticoagulant.
A.white blood cell count   B.nosocomial infection   C.citrate phosphate dextrose   D.collateral circulation

7. ____ Outside the living body; inside a glass; observable in a test tube.
A.fibrin   B.circulatory system   C.invitro   D.invivo

8. ____ A technique in which blood products are separated from a donor and the desired elements collected and the rest returned to the donor.
A.peritoneal dialysis   B.hypersensitivity   C.apheresis   D.cephalic vein

9. ____ Pertaining to the veins, or blood passing through them.
A.blood count   B.peritoneal dialysis   C.venous   D.efferent

10. ____ Nearest to any other point of reference.
A.hypodermic needle   B.proximal   C.whole blood   D.lymph

11. ____ To attract and retain other material on the surface.
A.artery   B.aseptic technique   C.thrombus   D.adsorb

12. ____ Any of the many forms of mononuclear phagocytes found in tissues and originating from stem cells in the bone marrow. In normal circulation, the monocyte may be categorized as a macrophage.
A.basilic vein   B.hematoma   C.artery   D.macrophage

13. ____ Blood from which none of the elements have been removed.
A.blood vessel   B.transmission based precautions   C.whole blood   D.antihemophilic factor

14. ____ Pertaining to the front side of the body.
A.ventral   B.vasoconstriction   C.peripheral blood   D.capillary

15. ____ A bruise or ""contusion" is a traumatic injury of the soft tissues which results in breakage of the local capillaries and leakage of red blood cells.
A.anticoagulant   B.peritoneal dialysis   C.bruise   D.thrombosis

16. ____ The circulatory system is composed of the heart, arteries, capillaries and veins.
A.distal   B.flexion   C.engineering control   D.circulatory system

17. ____ The cause or origin of a disease or disorder.
    A.proximal B.etiology C.nosocomial infection D.antiseptic

18. ____ A tube for insertion into a duct or cavity.
    A.cannula B.dorsal C.phagocytosis D.hepatitis a

19. ____ Pertaining to the palm or sole; indicating the flexor portion of the forearm, wrist or hand.
    A.pipet B.bloodletting C.germicide D.volar

20. ____ Carrying away. An artery is an efferent vessel carrying blood away from the heart.
    A.efferent B.anaphylaxis C.cephalic vein D.differential

21. ____ Dialysis through the peritoneum.
    A.complete blood count B.lymph C.citrate phosphate dextrose D.peritoneal dialysis

22. ____ A large vein of the arm that empties into the axillary vein
    A.distal B.povidone iodine C.autohemolysis D.cephalic vein

23. ____ The incision of a vein as for blood-letting (venesection); needle puncture of a vein for drawing blood (venipuncture).
    A.ecchymosis B.bloodletting C.macrophage D.phlebotomy

24. ____ One who practices phlebotomy.
    A.phlebotomist B.cannula C.bleeding time D.etiology

25. ____ Large vein on the inner side of the biceps. Often chosen for intravenous injections and blood drawing.
    A.basilic vein B.prophylaxis C.povidone iodine D.anticoagulant

26. ____ A state in which the body reacts with an exaggerated immune response to a foreign substance. Reactions are classified as delayed or immediate types.
    A.ecchymosis B.arteriole C.hypersensitivity D.edta

27. ____ A needle that attaches to a syringe for injections or withdrawal of fluids such as blood.
    A.anaerobic B.aspirate C.hypodermic needle D.blood film

28. ____ A semisolid mass of blood found inside or outside the body.
    A.dorsal B.vasoconstriction C.hypersensitivity D.clot

29. ____ The formation of a blood clot (thrombus) within a vessel.
    A.thrombosis B.invivo C.povidone iodine D.prophylaxis

30. ____ Situated at the back (dorsal) part of a structure.
    A.centrifuge B.circulatory system C.posterior D.arteriovenous fistula

31. ____ Growing, living or occurring in the absence of molecular oxygen; pertaining to an anaerobe.
    A.electrolyte B.fibrin C.anaerobic D.capillary

32. ____ Main protein in human blood.
    A.platelet B.standard precautions C.albumin D.anaerobic

33. ____ The determination of the proper number of red blood cells, white blood cells and platelets are present in the patient's blood.
    A.hepatitis a B.blood count C.antiseptic D.phagocytosis

34. ____ An agent that kills pathogenic microorganisms
    A.citrate phosphate dextrose B.prophylaxis C.phlebotomy D.germicide

35. ____ Pertaining to elements dissolved in blood or body fluids, e.g., homoral immunity from antibodies in the blood as opposed to cellular immunity.
A.germicide   B.aseptic technique   C.humoral   D.edta

36. ____ Fluid found in lymphatic vessels and nodes derived from tissue fluids. Lymph is collected from all parts of the body and returned to the blood by the lymphatic system.
A.collateral circulation   B.arteriole   C.lymph   D.circulatory system

37. ____ An abnormally low glucose level in the blood.
A.cannula   B.hepatitis a   C.contusion   D.hypoglycemia

38. ____ A count made on a stained blood smear of the proportion of the different leukocytes (WBC's) and expressed as a percentage.
A.invitro   B.differential   C.dorsal   D.white blood cell count

39. ____ That part of the arm opposing the elbow.
A.anaerobic   B.antecubital fossa   C.aseptic technique   D.proximal

40. ____ Cells that carry oxygen to all parts of the body.
A.erythrocyte   B.centrifuge   C.vascular graft   D.hematoma

41. ____ The number of white blood cells (leukocytes) found in the peripheral blood and measured per cubic millimeter.
A.anaphylaxis   B.serum   C.complete blood count   D.white blood cell count

42. ____ All the vessels lined with endothelium through which blood circulates.
A.heparin   B.reverse isolation   C.blood vessel   D.hypodermic needle

43. ____ A type of an arteriovenous fistula consisting of either a venous autograft or synthetic tube which is grafted to the artery and vein.
A.etiology   B.apheresis   C.vascular graft   D.antiseptic

44. ____ The protein formed during normal blood clotting that is the essence of the clot.
A.blood count   B.blood film   C.artery   D.fibrin

45. ____ The process of bending or the state of being bent. Flexion of the fingers results in a clenched fist.
A.hemoglobin   B.fibrin   C.basilic vein   D.flexion

46. ____ The selective separation and removal of platelets from withdrawn blood. The remainder of the blood is re-transfused back into the donor.
A.germicide   B.plateletpheresis   C.nosocomial infection   D.blood vessel

47. ____ A safety device designed to transfer blood from one container into another.
A.dorsal   B.edema   C.blood transfer device   D.white blood cell count

48. ____ Inflammation of a vein. The condition is marked by infiltration of the layers of the vein and the formation of a clot. It produces edema, stiffness and pain in the affected area.
A.pipet   B.reverse isolation   C.phlebitis   D.plasma

49. ____ Something that discourages the growth microorganisms. By contrast, aseptic refers to the absence of microorganisms.
A.prophylaxis   B.antiseptic   C.heparin   D.arteriovenous fistula

50. ____ Also known as a thrombocyte, this is a particulate component of the blood known for its involvement in blood coagulation.
A.reverse isolation   B.peritoneal dialysis   C.hypoglycemia   D.platelet

51. ____ An anticoagulant that acts to inhibit coagulation factors, especially factor Xa. Heparin is formed in the liver.
A.peritoneal dialysis B.ventral C.endothelium D.heparin

52. ____ Precautions that are designed for the care of all patients in hospitals regardless of their diagnosis or presumed infection status.
A.edema B.phlebotomist C.ecchymosis D.standard precautions

53. ____ The presence of viable bacteria circulating in the bloodstream. Diagnosed with blood cultures.
A.bacteremia B.differential C.phlebotomy D.capillary

54. ____ A method used by microbiologists and clinicians to keep cultures, sterile instruments and media, and people free of microbial contamination.
A.aseptic technique B.venous C.serum D.artery

55. ____ Blood obtained from the circulation away from the heart, such as from the fingertip, heel pad, earlobe or from an antecubital vein.
A.posterior B.peripheral blood C.venule D.venous

56. ____ A process where polymorphonuclear leukocytes, monocytes, and macrophages combine with lysosomes within the cell cytoplasm to digest and destroy a particulate.
A.contusion B.povidone iodine C.plateletpheresis D.phagocytosis

57. ____ A decrease in the inside diameter of especially arterioles leading to a decrease in blood flow to a part.
A.bloodletting B.engineering control C.vasoconstriction D.pipet

58. ____ Blood which infuses an area through a secondary or accessory route.
A.thrombus B.collateral circulation C.erythrocyte D.hypodermic needle

59. ____ Any substance that prevents blood clotting.
A.etiology B.anticoagulant C.blood vessel D.cannula

60. ____ A test which measures the time it takes for small blood vessels to close off and bleeding to stop.
A.povidone iodine B.bleeding time C.thrombus D.antihemophilic factor

61. ____ The state of the body early in the morning, approximately 12 hours after the last ingestion of food or other nutrition.
A.absorb B.autohemolysis C.basal state D.bacteremia

62. ____ A very tiny vein, continuous with the capillaries. Compare with arteriole.
A.efferent B.autohemolysis C.venule D.blood transfer device

63. ____ The ratio of the total red blood cell volume to the total blood volume and expressed as a percentage.
A.cephalic vein B.vacutainer C.hematocrit D.phagocytosis

64. ____ Inside the living body.
A.invivo B.edema C.syringe D.phlebitis

65. ____ Remote, farther from any point of reference, opposed to proximal
A.aspirate B.albumin C.distal D.hematoma

66. ____ Any one of the minute vessels that connect the arterioles and venules, forming a network in nearly all parts of the body.
A.phagocytosis B.capillary C.humoral D.dorsal

67. ____ The skin discoloration caused by a bruise (contusion).
A.ecchymosis B.aseptic technique C.hepatitis a D.bacteremia

68. ____ A sample of blood is applied to a microscope slide and then studied under the microscope.
A.adsorb B.albumin C.blood film D.peripheral blood

69. ____ An instrument used to inject fluids into or aspirate fluids from any vessel or cavity.
A.dorsal B.syringe C.plateletpheresis D.ecchymosis

70. ____ A hospital-borne infection. An infection whose origin is from within the hospital environment.
A.hypersensitivity B.absorb C.nosocomial infection D.invitro

71. ____ A mononuclear, phagocytic leukocyte.
A.white blood cell count B.engineering control C.blood vessel D.monocyte

72. ____ A category used for patients known or suspected to be infected or colonized with important pathogens.
A.phagocytosis B.edta C.vascular graft D.transmission based precautions

73. ____ Blood vessel carrying blood away from the heart. Arterial blood is normally full of oxygen.
A.medial B.cephalic vein C.vascular graft D.artery

74. ____ White blood cells.
A.efferent B.ecchymosis C.white blood cell count D.leukocyte

75. ____ Denoting a position more toward the back surface than some other object of reference; same as posterior in human anatomy.
A.differential B.dorsal C.absorb D.basal state

76. ____ A blood clot obstructing a blood vessel or a cavity of the heart. Heparin and Warfarin Sodium are being used to assist in dissolving or preventing clot formations.
A.basilic vein B.apheresis C.antecubital fossa D.thrombus

77. ____ An acute, generalized life-threatening allergic or hypersensitive reaction.
A.proximal B.vascular graft C.venule D.anaphylaxis

78. ____ A trade name now a generic term used to describe equipment used to automatically aspirate blood from a vessel by venipuncture.
A.blood transfer device B.vacutainer C.flexion D.phlebotomy

79. ____ The oxygen carrying pigment of the red blood cells.
A.vascular graft B.ecchymosis C.hemoglobin D.hypersensitivity

80. ____ Hemolysis of red blood cells of a person by his own serum.
A.aspirate B.plateletpheresis C.autohemolysis D.phagocytosis

81. ____ A type of coagulation (clotting) factors.
A.antiseptic B.bacteremia C.antihemophilic factor D.whole blood

82. ____ A laboratory apparatus that separates mixed samples into homogenous component layers by spinning them at high speed.
A.lymph B.citrate phosphate dextrose C.centrifuge D.hematocrit

83. ____ A glass or transparent plastic tube used to accurately measure small amounts of liquid.
A.hemoglobin B.proximal C.pipet D.anticoagulant

84. ____ Pertaining to the middle aspect; closer to the midline of the body or structure.
A.artery B.medial C.bacteremia D.anaphylaxis

85. ____ The act or process of letting blood or bleeding, as by opening a vein or artery, or by cupping or leeches.
A.germicide   B.absorb   C.electrolyte   D.bloodletting

86. ____ The fluid portion of the blood in which the cellular components are suspended. Plasma contains coagulation factors used in the clotting of blood as opposed to serum.
A.plasma   B.artery   C.endothelium   D.aseptic technique

87. ____ To suck up, as through pores.
A.flexion   B.differential   C.lymph   D.absorb

88. ____ A hollow silicone (soft, rubber-like material) tube inserted and secured into a large vein in the chest for long-term use to administer drugs or nutrients.
A.hickman catheter   B.distal   C.vascular graft   D.circulatory system

89. ____ A small branch of an artery that leads to a capillary. Also, see capillary.
A.arteriole   B.reverse isolation   C.basilic vein   D.contusion

90. ____ Controls (e.g., sharps disposal containers, self-sheathing needles) that isolate or remove the bloodborne pathogens hazard from the workplace.
A.engineering control   B.thrombus   C.blood film   D.ecchymosis

91. ____ The surgical joining of an artery and a vein under the skin for hemodialysis.
A.ventral   B.pipet   C.ecchymosis   D.arteriovenous fistula

92. ____ A substance that will acquire the capacity to conduct electricity when put into solution.
A.blood film   B.electrolyte   C.povidone iodine   D.aseptic technique

93. ____ A calcium chelating (binding) agent that is used as an anticoagulant for laboratory blood specimens. Also used in treatment of lead poisoning.
A.blood count   B.hypersensitivity   C.phlebotomist   D.edta

94. ____ The layer of cells lining the closed internal spaces of the body such as the blood vessels and lymphatic vessels.
A.posterior   B.circulatory system   C.endothelium   D.autohemolysis

95. ____ Usually a self-limited viral disease. Transmission is usually the result of poor hygiene and most often through the fecal-oral route.
A.hepatitis a   B.peripheral blood   C.engineering control   D.germicide

96. ____ An isolation procedure designed to protect the patient from contracting disease. Frequently used for transplant patients or for patients whose immune response has been greatly reduced.
A.arteriole   B.reverse isolation   C.ventral   D.anticoagulant

97. ____ A bruise or injury without a break in the skin.
A.nosocomial infection   B.contusion   C.blood count   D.adsorb

98. ____ Used as a topical antiseptic, this is a compound made by reacting iodine with povidone which slowly releases iodine.
A.monocyte   B.proximal   C.povidone iodine   D.invivo

99. ____ A preventative treatment.
A.hypoglycemia   B.bloodletting   C.prophylaxis   D.macrophage

100. ____ The number of red blood cells, white blood cells and platelets (per cubic millimeter) that are present in the patient's sample of blood is determined.
A.complete blood count   B.proximal   C.macrophage   D.ecchymosis

From the words provided for each clue, provide the letter of the word which best matches the clue.

101. ____ An anticoagulant that acts to inhibit coagulation factors, especially factor Xa. Heparin is formed in the liver.
A.fibrinogen B.leukocyte C.humoral D.heparin

102. ____ A decrease in the fluid content of the blood (plasma), resulting in an increase in concentration. This is determined by an increase in the hematocrit. Caused by a filtration of plasma into body tissues and often created by dehydration.
A.edema B.blood transfer device C.flexion D.hemoconcentration

103. ____ The soiling by inferior material, as by the introduction of organisms into a wound.
A.flexion B.fibrinogen C.contamination D.etiology

104. ____ In epidemiology, a group of individuals who share common characteristics.
A.ecchymosis B.cohorting C.bloodborne pathogens D.apheresis

105. ____ A thin film of paraffin used primarily in the laboratory to seal open containers such as test tubes.
A.acute B.phlebitis C.parafilm D.disinfectant

106. ____ Needle diameter is measured by gauge; the larger the needle diameter, the smaller the gauge.
A.phagocytosis B.macrophage C.blood D.gauge

107. ____ Any of the many forms of mononuclear phagocytes found in tissues and originating from stem cells in the bone marrow. In normal circulation, the monocyte may be categorized as a macrophage.
A.bloodborne pathogens B.pathogen C.contact precautions D.macrophage

108. ____ The process of bending or the state of being bent. Flexion of the fingers results in a clenched fist.
A.vascular graft B.venous C.flexion D.universal precautions

109. ____ A molecule that has a specific affinity for and reacts with the antigen that was responsible for its production or with one which is closely related.
A.thrombus B.blood vessel C.order of draw D.antibody

110. ____ This precaution is for specified patients known or suspected to be infected or colonized with microorganisms that can be transmitted by direct contact with the patient.
A.carbamate hemoglobin B.povidone iodine C.contact precautions D.acute

111. ____ The condition of having less than the normal number of red blood cells or hemoglobin in the blood.
A.differential B.anemia C.hypersensitivity D.allergen

112. ____ A set of procedures and protocols designed to protect the healthcare worker which uses the basic concept that each patient must be treated as though they were infected with an infectious disease.
A.posterior B.cephalic vein C.universal precautions D.prophylaxis

113. ____ All the vessels lined with endothelium through which blood circulates.
A.hypodermic needle B.blood vessel C.bleeding time D.thrombosis

114. ____ The incision of a vein as for blood-letting (venesection); needle puncture of a vein for drawing blood (venipuncture).
A.venous B.adsorb C.phlebotomy D.epidemiology

115. ____ Also known as a platelet, this is a particulate component of the blood, approximately 2-4 microns in diameter and known for its involvement in blood coagulation.
A.contact precautions B.thrombocyte C.monocyte D.blood culture

116. ___ The fluid in the body that contains red cells and white cells as well as platelets, proteins, plasma and other elements. It is transported throughout the body by the Circulatory System.
A.povidone iodine B.blood C.ecchymosis D.vascular graft

117. ___ A very tiny vein, continuous with the capillaries. Compare with arteriole.
A.complete blood count B.venule C.anemia D.carbamate hemoglobin

118. ___ An antigenic substance capable of producing an immediate-type hypersensitivity (allergy).
A.allergen B.anesthetic C.palmar D.bleeding time

119. ___ The outside layer of cells that covers all the free, open surfaces of the body including the skin, and mucous membranes that communicate with the outside of the body.
A.harvesting B.parafilm C.epithelium D.universal precautions

120. ___ A method used by microbiologists and clinicians to keep cultures, sterile instruments and media, and people free of microbial contamination.
A.blood count B.allergen C.aseptic technique D.nosocomial infection

121. ___ Inflammation of a vein. The condition is marked by infiltration of the layers of the vein and the formation of a clot. It produces edema, stiffness and pain in the affected area.
A.blood cell B.order of draw C.antigen D.phlebitis

122. ___ Terminology used to define the order in which blood sample tubes should be drawn using a multi-sample technique such as the Vacutainer System.
A.blood B.order of draw C.bleeding time D.engineering control

123. ___ Used as a topical antiseptic, this is a compound made by reacting iodine with povidone which slowly releases iodine.
A.engineering control B.fibrinogen C.macrophage D.povidone iodine

124. ___ Pertaining to elements dissolved in blood or body fluids, e.g., homoral immunity from antibodies in the blood as opposed to cellular immunity.
A.vascular B.humoral C.venule D.flexion

125. ___ An implant or transplant of any tissue or organ.
A.hemoconcentration B.cefibrinated blood C.aspirate D.graft

126. ___ A type of coagulation (clotting) factors.
A.aseptic technique B.bloodborne pathogens C.antihemophilic factor D.anesthetic

127. ___ The upper or outer layer of the two main layers of cells that make up the skin.
A.epidermis B.graft C.aspirate D.adsorb

128. ___ The science concerned with the study of factors influencing the distribution of disease and their causes in a defined population.
A.epidemiology B.hypersensitivity C.heparin D.macrophage

129. ___ The hemoglobin compound bound with carbon dioxide in the red blood cells.
A.warfarin sodium B.monocyte C.carbamate hemoglobin D.epidemiology

130. ___ A preventative treatment.
A.adsorb B.etiology C.monocyte D.prophylaxis

131. ___ The swelling of soft tissues caused by excess fluid accumulation.
A.coagulation factors B.pathogenic C.edema D.antiseptic

132. ____ There are three main types of cell in the blood stream. The red cell, which carries oxygen, the white cell, which fights infections and the platelet, which helps prevent bleeding.
A.macrophage B.blood transfer device C.universal precautions D.blood cell

133. ____ Called White Blood Cells. A variety of cells within the blood and bone marrow whose general purpose is to help in fighting infection.
A.cefibrinated blood B.macrophage C.leukocyte D.hemoconcentration

134. ____ A technique in which blood products are separated from a donor and the desired elements collected and the rest returned to the donor.
A.etiology B.chelate C.apheresis D.faint

135. ____ An abnormally low glucose level in the blood.
A.hypoglycemia B.venous C.harvesting D.parafilm

136. ____ An agent that disinfects, applied particularly to agents used on inanimate objects.
A.aspirate B.blood culture C.absorb D.disinfectant

137. ____ The number of red blood cells, white blood cells and platelets (per cubic millimeter) that are present in the patient's sample of blood is determined.
A.anemia B.epithelium C.distal D.complete blood count

138. ____ A sudden loss of consciousness.
A.venous B.absorb C.faint D.flexion

139. ____ A test which measures the time it takes for small blood vessels to close off and bleeding to stop.
A.mean corpuscular volume B.antigen C.bleeding time D.disinfectant

140. ____ A safety device designed to transfer blood from one container into another.
A.blood transfer device B.blood C.coagulation factors D.fibrinogen

141. ____ A test which involves the incubation of a blood specimen overnight to determine if bacteria are present.
A.proximal B.absorb C.blood culture D.carbamate hemoglobin

142. ____ Of short duration. Rapid and abbreviated in onset.
A.thrombocytopenia B.proximal C.acute D.nosocomial infection

143. ____ Pertaining to the veins, or blood passing through them.
A.hypodermic needle B.diaphoretic C.blood culture D.venous

144. ____ The protein from which fibrin is formed.
A.fibrinogen B.allergen C.chromatin D.warfarin sodium

145. ____ A process where polymorphonuclear leukocytes, monocytes, and macrophages combine with lysosomes within the cell cytoplasm to digest and destroy a particulate.
A.blood B.universal precautions C.phagocytosis D.vacutainer tube

146. ____ Large vein on the inner side of the biceps. Often chosen for intravenous injections and blood drawing.
A.distal B.basilic vein C.collateral circulation D.epithelium

147. ____ Having the capability of producing disease.
A.ecchymosis B.apheresis C.universal precautions D.pathogenic

148. ____ White blood cells.
A.acute B.leukocyte C.antihemophilic factor D.circulation

149. ___ Referring to the palm surface or side of the hand
A.edema   B.palmar   C.cohorting   D.red blood cell

150. ___ The membrane lining the abdominal and pelvic wall.
A.pathogenic   B.engineering control   C.peritoneum   D.apheresis

151. ___ A hospital-borne infection. An infection whose origin is from within the hospital environment.
A.nosocomial infection   B.pathogen   C.epithelium   D.circulation

152. ___ Blood sample tubes containing a vacuum. When the tube stopper is pierced by a Vacutainer needle which has been properly positioned in a vein, the vacuum draws blood into the tube.
A.chelate   B.vacutainer tube   C.blood   D.antibody

153. ___ As it relates to blood drawing, the material that is withdrawn with a negative pressure apparatus (syringe).
A.diaphoretic   B.adsorb   C.aspirate   D.citrate phosphate dextrose

154. ___ Something that discourages the growth microorganisms. By contrast, aseptic refers to the absence of microorganisms.
A.vacutainer   B.antiseptic   C.thrombocyte   D.basal state

155. ___ Formation of profuse perspiration (sweat). A symptom of syncope or vasovagal response.
A.pathogenic   B.universal precautions   C.leukocyte   D.diaphoretic

156. ___ The component of the blood that contains hemoglobin which is responsible for oxygen and carbon dioxide exchange.
A.antihemophilic factor   B.pathogenic   C.epidemiology   D.red blood cell

157. ___ Blood vessels carrying blood to the heart. Blood contained within these vessels is generally bound with carbon dioxide which will be exchanged for oxygen in the lungs.
A.vein   B.allergen   C.red blood cell   D.basal state

158. ___ To suck up, as through pores.
A.hemoconcentration   B.anesthetic   C.absorb   D.leukocyte

159. ___ Any microorganism that produces disease.
A.pathogen   B.vacutainer   C.cefibrinated blood   D.basal state

160. ___ A type of an arteriovenous fistula consisting of either a venous autograft or synthetic tube which is grafted to the artery and vein.
A.hypersensitivity   B.peritoneum   C.vascular graft   D.diaphoretic

161. ___ Precautions that are designed for the care of all patients in hospitals regardless of their diagnosis or presumed infection status.
A.cohorting   B.standard precautions   C.hemolysis   D.flexion

162. ___ An anticoagulant.
A.vascular graft   B.vacutainer   C.flexion   D.citrate phosphate dextrose

163. ___ The more readily stainable portion of the cell nucleus. It is a DNA attached to a protein structure and is the carrier of genes in inheritance.
A.macrophage   B.chromatin   C.hypodermic needle   D.basilic vein

164. ___ Average volume of red blood cells.
A.apheresis   B.complete blood count   C.mean corpuscular volume   D.venous

165. ___ Remote, farther from any point of reference, opposed to proximal
A.heparin   B.contamination   C.collateral circulation   D.distal

166. ____ The breaking of the red blood cells membrane releasing free hemoglobin into the circulating blood.
A.epidemiology   B.prophylaxis   C.hemolysis   D.vacutainer tube

167. ____ Combining with a metallic ion into a ring complex.
A.chelate   B.thrombus   C.blood group   D.edema

168. ____ To examine or feel by the hand. In relation to venipunctures, this technique is used to "feel" a vein which will tend to rebound when slight pressure is applied with the finger.
A.monocyte   B.palpate   C.antiseptic   D.differential

169. ____ Pertaining to or composed of blood vessels. The vascular system is composed of the heart, blood vessels, lymphatics and their parts considered collectively.
A.vacutainer tube   B.differential   C.antihemophilic factor   D.vascular

170. ____ Decrease in the number of blood platelets below normal values.
A.allergen   B.povidone iodine   C.thrombocytopenia   D.blood group

171. ____ Controls (e.g., sharps disposal containers, self-sheathing needles) that isolate or remove the bloodborne pathogens hazard from the workplace.
A.vascular graft   B.edema   C.engineering control   D.leukocyte

172. ____ An abnormal passageway usually between two internal organs. Such passages may be created experimentally for obtaining body secretions for study.
A.fistula   B.palmar   C.blood vessel   D.antigen

173. ____ An object or material, such as tissue, partially or totally inserted or grafted into the body of a recipient.
A.antigen   B.citrate phosphate dextrose   C.implant   D.parafilm

174. ____ The cause or origin of a disease or disorder.
A.heparin   B.etiology   C.nosocomial infection   D.ecchymosis

175. ____ A needle that attaches to a syringe for injections or withdrawal of fluids such as blood.
A.harvesting   B.hypodermic needle   C.aseptic technique   D.phlebitis

176. ____ The movement of fluid in a regular or circuitous course.
A.disinfectant   B.blood culture   C.collateral circulation   D.circulation

177. ____ A count made on a stained blood smear of the proportion of the different leukocytes (WBC's) and expressed as a percentage.
A.differential   B.heparin   C.absorb   D.edema

178. ____ The oxygen carrying pigment of the red blood cells.
A.circulation   B.hemoglobin   C.red blood cell   D.distal

179. ____ A substance capable of producing a specific immune response with a specific antibody.
A.allergen   B.hemolysis   C.antigen   D.coagulation factors

180. ____ A blood clot obstructing a blood vessel or a cavity of the heart. Heparin and Warfarin Sodium are being used to assist in dissolving or preventing clot formations.
A.red blood cell   B.nosocomial infection   C.anemia   D.thrombus

181. ____ Nearest to any other point of reference.
A.standard precautions   B.proximal   C.absorb   D.apheresis

182. ____ Blood which has been deprived of fibrin.
A.contamination   B.cohorting   C.cefibrinated blood   D.blood group

183. ____ The state of the body early in the morning, approximately 12 hours after the last ingestion of food or other nutrition.
A.order of draw B.palmar C.basal state D.monocyte

184. ____ The collection and preservation of tissues or cells from a donor for transplantation.
A.chelate B.antihemophilic factor C.harvesting D.implant

185. ____ An inherited feature on the surface of the red blood cell. A series of related blood groups make up a blood group system such as the ABO system or the Rh system.
A.blood group B.harvesting C.thrombus D.bloodborne pathogens

186. ____ To attract and retain other material on the surface.
A.thrombocytopenia B.red blood cell C.fistula D.adsorb

187. ____ A trade name now a generic term used to describe equipment used to automatically aspirate blood from a vessel by venipuncture.
A.thrombus B.vacutainer C.universal precautions D.monocyte

188. ____ The skin discoloration caused by a bruise (contusion).
A.ecchymosis B.diaphoretic C.venule D.hemolysis

189. ____ Group of plasma protein substances (Factor I thru XIII) contained in the plasma, which act together to bring about blood coagulation.
A.coagulation factors B.hemoglobin C.blood count D.red blood cell

190. ____ A hardening, especially from inflammation and certain disease states. Though sclerosis may occur in many areas of the body, the term is most often associated with blood vessels.
A.sclerosis B.citrate phosphate dextrose C.vascular graft D.leukocyte

191. ____ A mononuclear, phagocytic leukocyte.
A.nosocomial infection B.carbamate hemoglobin C.monocyte D.palmar

192. ____ The formation of a blood clot (thrombus) within a vessel.
A.blood culture B.thrombosis C.antiseptic D.bloodborne pathogens

193. ____ Any disease producing microorganism which is spread through direct contact with contaminated blood.
A.bloodborne pathogens B.cefibrinated blood C.blood D.complete blood count

194. ____ The sodium salt of warfarin, one of the synthetic anticoagulants. Coumadin is a brand name.
A.ecchymosis B.macrophage C.absorb D.warfarin sodium

195. ____ A state in which the body reacts with an exaggerated immune response to a foreign substance. Reactions are classified as delayed or immediate types.
A.hypersensitivity B.antigen C.absorb D.blood cell

196. ____ The determination of the proper number of red blood cells, white blood cells and platelets are present in the patient's blood.
A.sclerosis B.blood group C.blood count D.harvesting

197. ____ Blood which infuses an area through a secondary or accessory route.
A.cefibrinated blood B.collateral circulation C.apheresis D.basilic vein

198. ____ Situated at the back (dorsal) part of a structure.
A.blood cell B.proximal C.posterior D.phagocytosis

199. ____ A large vein of the arm that empties into the axillary vein
A.gauge B.cephalic vein C.fibrinogen D.acute

200. ___ A drug that causes unconsciousness or a loss of general sensation. A local anesthetic causes loss of feeling in a part of the body.
A.aseptic technique   B.anesthetic   C.leukocyte   D.epidermis

From the words provided for each clue, provide the letter of the word which best matches the clue.

201. ___ The surgical joining of an artery and a vein under the skin for hemodialysis.
A.fasting   B.supine   C.engineering control   D.arteriovenous fistula

202. ___ Fluid found in lymphatic vessels and nodes derived from tissue fluids. Lymph is collected from all parts of the body and returned to the blood by the lymphatic system.
A.fasting   B.syncope   C.lymph   D.vacutainer holder

203. ___ Also known as a platelet, this is a particulate component of the blood, approximately 2-4 microns in diameter and known for its involvement in blood coagulation.
A.arteriovenous fistula   B.hemoconcentration   C.faint   D.thrombocyte

204. ___ The cause or origin of a disease or disorder.
A.pathogenic   B.heparin   C.etiology   D.vacutainer holder

205. ___ Fainting; a temporary loss of consciousness due to a reduction of blood to the brain.
A.vacutainer holder   B.lymph   C.syncope   D.engineering control

206. ___ Having the capability of producing disease.
A.lymph   B.hemoconcentration   C.pathogenic   D.contagious

207. ___ There are three main types of cell in the blood stream. The red cell, which carries oxygen, the white cell, which fights infections and the platelet, which helps prevent bleeding.
A.blood cell   B.pathogenic   C.engineering control   D.supine

208. ___ Infectious. May be transmitted from person to person.
A.contagious   B.lymph   C.thrombocyte   D.blood cell

209. ___ Lying down with the face up; opposed to prone.
A.supine   B.hemoconcentration   C.vacutainer holder   D.fasting

210. ___ Without eating. Some laboratory tests are performed on "fasting" blood specimens such as sugar (glucose) levels and tolerance tests such as glucose, lactose and dextrose.
A.thrombocyte   B.pathogenic   C.fasting   D.vacutainer holder

211. ___ An anticoagulant that acts to inhibit coagulation factors, especially factor Xa. Heparin is formed in the liver.
A.lymph   B.heparin   C.etiology   D.thrombocyte

212. ___ A cylindrical shaped holder that accepts a Vacutainer tube on one end and a Vacutainer needle on the other.
A.lymph   B.etiology   C.vacutainer holder   D.thrombocyte

213. ___ A decrease in the fluid content of the blood (plasma), resulting in an increase in concentration. This is determined by an increase in the hematocrit. Caused by a filtration of plasma into body tissues and often created by dehydration.
A.pathogenic   B.hemoconcentration   C.faint   D.blood cell

214. ___ Controls (e.g., sharps disposal containers, self-sheathing needles) that isolate or remove the bloodborne pathogens hazard from the workplace.
A.supine   B.lymph   C.arteriovenous fistula   D.engineering control

215. ___ A sudden loss of consciousness.
A.fasting   B.faint   C.contagious   D.pathogenic

From the words provided for each clue, provide the letter of the word which best matches the clue.

1. __D__ A localized collection of blood within tissue due to leakage from the wall of a blood vessel, producing a bluish discoloration (ecchymosis)and pain.
   A.aseptic technique   B.povidone iodine   C.adsorb   D.hematoma

2. __D__ As it relates to blood drawing, the material that is withdrawn with a negative pressure apparatus (syringe).
   A.hypersensitivity   B.aseptic technique   C.anticoagulant   D.aspirate

3. __C__ Referring to blood, the clear liquid portion of blood that separates out after clotting has taken place. Since clotting has occurred, serum is fibrinogen deficient. Contrast to plasma.
   A.transmission based precautions   B.hypersensitivity   C.serum   D.anaphylaxis

4. __B__ The swelling of soft tissues caused by excess fluid accumulation.
   A.germicide   B.edema   C.basal state   D.nosocomial infection

5. __B__ Performing a venipuncture with no apparently visible or palpable vein.
   A.vascular graft   B.blind stick   C.erythrocyte   D.whole blood

6. __C__ An anticoagulant.
   A.white blood cell count   B.nosocomial infection   C.citrate phosphate dextrose   D.collateral circulation

7. __C__ Outside the living body; inside a glass; observable in a test tube.
   A.fibrin   B.circulatory system   C.invitro   D.invivo

8. __C__ A technique in which blood products are separated from a donor and the desired elements collected and the rest returned to the donor.
   A.peritoneal dialysis   B.hypersensitivity   C.apheresis   D.cephalic vein

9. __C__ Pertaining to the veins, or blood passing through them.
   A.blood count   B.peritoneal dialysis   C.venous   D.efferent

10. __B__ Nearest to any other point of reference.
    A.hypodermic needle   B.proximal   C.whole blood   D.lymph

11. __D__ To attract and retain other material on the surface.
    A.artery   B.aseptic technique   C.thrombus   D.adsorb

12. __D__ Any of the many forms of mononuclear phagocytes found in tissues and originating from stem cells in the bone marrow. In normal circulation, the monocyte may be categorized as a macrophage.
    A.basilic vein   B.hematoma   C.artery   D.macrophage

13. __C__ Blood from which none of the elements have been removed.
    A.blood vessel   B.transmission based precautions   C.whole blood   D.antihemophilic factor

14. __A__ Pertaining to the front side of the body.
    A.ventral   B.vasoconstriction   C.peripheral blood   D.capillary

15. __C__ A bruise or ""contusion" is a traumatic injury of the soft tissues which results in breakage of the local capillaries and leakage of red blood cells.
    A.anticoagulant   B.peritoneal dialysis   C.bruise   D.thrombosis

16. __D__ The circulatory system is composed of the heart, arteries, capillaries and veins.
    A.distal   B.flexion   C.engineering control   D.circulatory system

17. B   The cause or origin of a disease or disorder.
        A.proximal   B.etiology   C.nosocomial infection   D.antiseptic

18. A   A tube for insertion into a duct or cavity.
        A.cannula   B.dorsal   C.phagocytosis   D.hepatitis a

19. D   Pertaining to the palm or sole; indicating the flexor portion of the forearm, wrist or hand.
        A.pipet   B.bloodletting   C.germicide   D.volar

20. A   Carrying away. An artery is an efferent vessel carrying blood away from the heart.
        A.efferent   B.anaphylaxis   C.cephalic vein   D.differential

21. D   Dialysis through the peritoneum.
        A.complete blood count   B.lymph   C.citrate phosphate dextrose   D.peritoneal dialysis

22. D   A large vein of the arm that empties into the axillary vein
        A.distal   B.povidone iodine   C.autohemolysis   D.cephalic vein

23. D   The incision of a vein as for blood-letting (venesection); needle puncture of a vein for drawing blood (venipuncture).
        A.ecchymosis   B.bloodletting   C.macrophage   D.phlebotomy

24. A   One who practices phlebotomy.
        A.phlebotomist   B.cannula   C.bleeding time   D.etiology

25. A   Large vein on the inner side of the biceps. Often chosen for intravenous injections and blood drawing.
        A.basilic vein   B.prophylaxis   C.povidone iodine   D.anticoagulant

26. C   A state in which the body reacts with an exaggerated immune response to a foreign substance. Reactions are classified as delayed or immediate types.
        A.ecchymosis   B.arteriole   C.hypersensitivity   D.edta

27. C   A needle that attaches to a syringe for injections or withdrawal of fluids such as blood.
        A.anaerobic   B.aspirate   C.hypodermic needle   D.blood film

28. D   A semisolid mass of blood found inside or outside the body.
        A.dorsal   B.vasoconstriction   C.hypersensitivity   D.clot

29. A   The formation of a blood clot (thrombus) within a vessel.
        A.thrombosis   B.invivo   C.povidone iodine   D.prophylaxis

30. C   Situated at the back (dorsal) part of a structure.
        A.centrifuge   B.circulatory system   C.posterior   D.arteriovenous fistula

31. C   Growing, living or occurring in the absence of molecular oxygen; pertaining to an anaerobe.
        A.electrolyte   B.fibrin   C.anaerobic   D.capillary

32. C   Main protein in human blood.
        A.platelet   B.standard precautions   C.albumin   D.anaerobic

33. B   The determination of the proper number of red blood cells, white blood cells and platelets are present in the patient's blood.
        A.hepatitis a   B.blood count   C.antiseptic   D.phagocytosis

34. D   An agent that kills pathogenic microorganisms
        A.citrate phosphate dextrose   B.prophylaxis   C.phlebotomy   D.germicide

35. C   Pertaining to elements dissolved in blood or body fluids, e.g., homoral immunity from antibodies in the blood as opposed to cellular immunity.
   A.germicide   B.aseptic technique   C.humoral   D.edta

36. C   Fluid found in lymphatic vessels and nodes derived from tissue fluids. Lymph is collected from all parts of the body and returned to the blood by the lymphatic system.
   A.collateral circulation   B.arteriole   C.lymph   D.circulatory system

37. D   An abnormally low glucose level in the blood.
   A.cannula   B.hepatitis a   C.contusion   D.hypoglycemia

38. B   A count made on a stained blood smear of the proportion of the different leukocytes (WBC's) and expressed as a percentage.
   A.invitro   B.differential   C.dorsal   D.white blood cell count

39. B   That part of the arm opposing the elbow.
   A.anaerobic   B.antecubital fossa   C.aseptic technique   D.proximal

40. A   Cells that carry oxygen to all parts of the body.
   A.erythrocyte   B.centrifuge   C.vascular graft   D.hematoma

41. D   The number of white blood cells (leukocytes) found in the peripheral blood and measured per cubic millimeter.
   A.anaphylaxis   B.serum   C.complete blood count   D.white blood cell count

42. C   All the vessels lined with endothelium through which blood circulates.
   A.heparin   B.reverse isolation   C.blood vessel   D.hypodermic needle

43. C   A type of an arteriovenous fistula consisting of either a venous autograft or synthetic tube which is grafted to the artery and vein.
   A.etiology   B.apheresis   C.vascular graft   D.antiseptic

44. D   The protein formed during normal blood clotting that is the essence of the clot.
   A.blood count   B.blood film   C.artery   D.fibrin

45. D   The process of bending or the state of being bent. Flexion of the fingers results in a clenched fist.
   A.hemoglobin   B.fibrin   C.basilic vein   D.flexion

46. B   The selective separation and removal of platelets from withdrawn blood. The remainder of the blood is re-transfused back into the donor.
   A.germicide   B.plateletpheresis   C.nosocomial infection   D.blood vessel

47. C   A safety device designed to transfer blood from one container into another.
   A.dorsal   B.edema   C.blood transfer device   D.white blood cell count

48. C   Inflammation of a vein. The condition is marked by infiltration of the layers of the vein and the formation of a clot. It produces edema, stiffness and pain in the affected area.
   A.pipet   B.reverse isolation   C.phlebitis   D.plasma

49. B   Something that discourages the growth microorganisms. By contrast, aseptic refers to the absence of microorganisms.
   A.prophylaxis   B.antiseptic   C.heparin   D.arteriovenous fistula

50. D   Also known as a thrombocyte, this is a particulate component of the blood known for its involvement in blood coagulation.
   A.reverse isolation   B.peritoneal dialysis   C.hypoglycemia   D.platelet

51. D   An anticoagulant that acts to inhibit coagulation factors, especially factor Xa. Heparin is formed in the liver.
A.peritoneal dialysis   B.ventral   C.endothelium   D.heparin

52. D   Precautions that are designed for the care of all patients in hospitals regardless of their diagnosis or presumed infection status.
A.edema   B.phlebotomist   C.ecchymosis   D.standard precautions

53. A   The presence of viable bacteria circulating in the bloodstream. Diagnosed with blood cultures.
A.bacteremia   B.differential   C.phlebotomy   D.capillary

54. A   A method used by microbiologists and clinicians to keep cultures, sterile instruments and media, and people free of microbial contamination.
A.aseptic technique   B.venous   C.serum   D.artery

55. B   Blood obtained from the circulation away from the heart, such as from the fingertip, heel pad, earlobe or from an antecubital vein.
A.posterior   B.peripheral blood   C.venule   D.venous

56. D   A process where polymorphonuclear leukocytes, monocytes, and macrophages combine with lysosomes within the cell cytoplasm to digest and destroy a particulate.
A.contusion   B.povidone iodine   C.plateletpheresis   D.phagocytosis

57. C   A decrease in the inside diameter of especially arterioles leading to a decrease in blood flow to a part.
A.bloodletting   B.engineering control   C.vasoconstriction   D.pipet

58. B   Blood which infuses an area through a secondary or accessory route.
A.thrombus   B.collateral circulation   C.erythrocyte   D.hypodermic needle

59. B   Any substance that prevents blood clotting.
A.etiology   B.anticoagulant   C.blood vessel   D.cannula

60. B   A test which measures the time it takes for small blood vessels to close off and bleeding to stop.
A.povidone iodine   B.bleeding time   C.thrombus   D.antihemophilic factor

61. C   The state of the body early in the morning, approximately 12 hours after the last ingestion of food or other nutrition.
A.absorb   B.autohemolysis   C.basal state   D.bacteremia

62. C   A very tiny vein, continuous with the capillaries. Compare with arteriole.
A.efferent   B.autohemolysis   C.venule   D.blood transfer device

63. C   The ratio of the total red blood cell volume to the total blood volume and expressed as a percentage.
A.cephalic vein   B.vacutainer   C.hematocrit   D.phagocytosis

64. A   Inside the living body.
A.invivo   B.edema   C.syringe   D.phlebitis

65. C   Remote, farther from any point of reference, opposed to proximal
A.aspirate   B.albumin   C.distal   D.hematoma

66. B   Any one of the minute vessels that connect the arterioles and venules, forming a network in nearly all parts of the body.
A.phagocytosis   B.capillary   C.humoral   D.dorsal

67. A   The skin discoloration caused by a bruise (contusion).
    A.ecchymosis B.aseptic technique C.hepatitis a D.bacteremia

68. C   A sample of blood is applied to a microscope slide and then studied under the microscope.
    A.adsorb B.albumin C.blood film D.peripheral blood

69. B   An instrument used to inject fluids into or aspirate fluids from any vessel or cavity.
    A.dorsal B.syringe C.plateletpheresis D.ecchymosis

70. C   A hospital-borne infection. An infection whose origin is from within the hospital environment.
    A.hypersensitivity B.absorb C.nosocomial infection D.invitro

71. D   A mononuclear, phagocytic leukocyte.
    A.white blood cell count B.engineering control C.blood vessel D.monocyte

72. D   A category used for patients known or suspected to be infected or colonized with important pathogens.
    A.phagocytosis B.edta C.vascular graft D.transmission based precautions

73. D   Blood vessel carrying blood away from the heart. Arterial blood is normally full of oxygen.
    A.medial B.cephalic vein C.vascular graft D.artery

74. D   White blood cells.
    A.efferent B.ecchymosis C.white blood cell count D.leukocyte

75. B   Denoting a position more toward the back surface than some other object of reference; same as posterior in human anatomy.
    A.differential B.dorsal C.absorb D.basal state

76. D   A blood clot obstructing a blood vessel or a cavity of the heart. Heparin and Warfarin Sodium are being used to assist in dissolving or preventing clot formations.
    A.basilic vein B.apheresis C.antecubital fossa D.thrombus

77. D   An acute, generalized life-threatening allergic or hypersensitive reaction.
    A.proximal B.vascular graft C.venule D.anaphylaxis

78. B   A trade name now a generic term used to describe equipment used to automatically aspirate blood from a vessel by venipuncture.
    A.blood transfer device B.vacutainer C.flexion D.phlebotomy

79. C   The oxygen carrying pigment of the red blood cells.
    A.vascular graft B.ecchymosis C.hemoglobin D.hypersensitivity

80. C   Hemolysis of red blood cells of a person by his own serum.
    A.aspirate B.plateletpheresis C.autohemolysis D.phagocytosis

81. C   A type of coagulation (clotting) factors.
    A.antiseptic B.bacteremia C.antihemophilic factor D.whole blood

82. C   A laboratory apparatus that separates mixed samples into homogenous component layers by spinning them at high speed.
    A.lymph B.citrate phosphate dextrose C.centrifuge D.hematocrit

83. C   A glass or transparent plastic tube used to accurately measure small amounts of liquid.
    A.hemoglobin B.proximal C.pipet D.anticoagulant

84. B   Pertaining to the middle aspect; closer to the midline of the body or structure.
    A.artery B.medial C.bacteremia D.anaphylaxis

85. D   The act or process of letting blood or bleeding, as by opening a vein or artery, or by cupping or leeches.
A.germicide B.absorb C.electrolyte D.bloodletting

86. A   The fluid portion of the blood in which the cellular components are suspended. Plasma contains coagulation factors used in the clotting of blood as opposed to serum.
A.plasma B.artery C.endothelium D.aseptic technique

87. D   To suck up, as through pores.
A.flexion B.differential C.lymph D.absorb

88. A   A hollow silicone (soft, rubber-like material) tube inserted and secured into a large vein in the chest for long-term use to administer drugs or nutrients.
A.hickman catheter B.distal C.vascular graft D.circulatory system

89. A   A small branch of an artery that leads to a capillary. Also, see capillary.
A.arteriole B.reverse isolation C.basilic vein D.contusion

90. A   Controls (e.g., sharps disposal containers, self-sheathing needles) that isolate or remove the bloodborne pathogens hazard from the workplace.
A.engineering control B.thrombus C.blood film D.ecchymosis

91. D   The surgical joining of an artery and a vein under the skin for hemodialysis.
A.ventral B.pipet C.ecchymosis D.arteriovenous fistula

92. B   A substance that will acquire the capacity to conduct electricity when put into solution.
A.blood film B.electrolyte C.povidone iodine D.aseptic technique

93. D   A calcium chelating (binding) agent that is used as an anticoagulant for laboratory blood specimens. Also used in treatment of lead poisoning.
A.blood count B.hypersensitivity C.phlebotomist D.edta

94. C   The layer of cells lining the closed internal spaces of the body such as the blood vessels and lymphatic vessels.
A.posterior B.circulatory system C.endothelium D.autohemolysis

95. A   Usually a self-limited viral disease. Transmission is usually the result of poor hygiene and most often through the fecal-oral route.
A.hepatitis a B.peripheral blood C.engineering control D.germicide

96. B   An isolation procedure designed to protect the patient from contracting disease. Frequently used for transplant patients or for patients whose immune response has been greatly reduced.
A.arteriole B.reverse isolation C.ventral D.anticoagulant

97. B   A bruise or injury without a break in the skin.
A.nosocomial infection B.contusion C.blood count D.adsorb

98. C   Used as a topical antiseptic, this is a compound made by reacting iodine with povidone which slowly releases iodine.
A.monocyte B.proximal C.povidone iodine D.invivo

99. C   A preventative treatment.
A.hypoglycemia B.bloodletting C.prophylaxis D.macrophage

100. A   The number of red blood cells, white blood cells and platelets (per cubic millimeter) that are present in the patient's sample of blood is determined.
A.complete blood count B.proximal C.macrophage D.ecchymosis

From the words provided for each clue, provide the letter of the word which best matches the clue.

101. D   An anticoagulant that acts to inhibit coagulation factors, especially factor Xa. Heparin is formed in the liver.
A.fibrinogen   B.leukocyte   C.humoral   D.heparin

102. D   A decrease in the fluid content of the blood (plasma), resulting in an increase in concentration. This is determined by an increase in the hematocrit. Caused by a filtration of plasma into body tissues and often created by dehydration.
A.edema   B.blood transfer device   C.flexion   D.hemoconcentration

103. C   The soiling by inferior material, as by the introduction of organisms into a wound.
A.flexion   B.fibrinogen   C.contamination   D.etiology

104. B   In epidemiology, a group of individuals who share common characteristics.
A.ecchymosis   B.cohorting   C.bloodborne pathogens   D.apheresis

105. C   A thin film of paraffin used primarily in the laboratory to seal open containers such as test tubes.
A.acute   B.phlebitis   C.parafilm   D.disinfectant

106. D   Needle diameter is measured by gauge; the larger the needle diameter, the smaller the gauge.
A.phagocytosis   B.macrophage   C.blood   D.gauge

107. D   Any of the many forms of mononuclear phagocytes found in tissues and originating from stem cells in the bone marrow. In normal circulation, the monocyte may be categorized as a macrophage.
A.bloodborne pathogens   B.pathogen   C.contact precautions   D.macrophage

108. C   The process of bending or the state of being bent. Flexion of the fingers results in a clenched fist.
A.vascular graft   B.venous   C.flexion   D.universal precautions

109. D   A molecule that has a specific affinity for and reacts with the antigen that was responsible for its production or with one which is closely related.
A.thrombus   B.blood vessel   C.order of draw   D.antibody

110. C   This precaution is for specified patients known or suspected to be infected or colonized with microorganisms that can be transmitted by direct contact with the patient.
A.carbamate hemoglobin   B.povidone iodine   C.contact precautions   D.acute

111. B   The condition of having less than the normal number of red blood cells or hemoglobin in the blood.
A.differential   B.anemia   C.hypersensitivity   D.allergen

112. C   A set of procedures and protocols designed to protect the healthcare worker which uses the basic concept that each patient must be treated as though they were infected with an infectious disease.
A.posterior   B.cephalic vein   C.universal precautions   D.prophylaxis

113. B   All the vessels lined with endothelium through which blood circulates.
A.hypodermic needle   B.blood vessel   C.bleeding time   D.thrombosis

114. C   The incision of a vein as for blood-letting (venesection); needle puncture of a vein for drawing blood (venipuncture).
A.venous   B.adsorb   C.phlebotomy   D.epidemiology

115. B   Also known as a platelet, this is a particulate component of the blood, approximately 2-4 microns in diameter and known for its involvement in blood coagulation.
A.contact precautions   B.thrombocyte   C.monocyte   D.blood culture

116. B   The fluid in the body that contains red cells and white cells as well as platelets, proteins, plasma and other elements. It is transported throughout the body by the Circulatory System.
A.povidone iodine   B.blood   C.ecchymosis   D.vascular graft

117. B   A very tiny vein, continuous with the capillaries. Compare with arteriole.
A.complete blood count   B.venule   C.anemia   D.carbamate hemoglobin

118. A   An antigenic substance capable of producing an immediate-type hypersensitivity (allergy).
A.allergen   B.anesthetic   C.palmar   D.bleeding time

119. C   The outside layer of cells that covers all the free, open surfaces of the body including the skin, and mucous membranes that communicate with the outside of the body.
A.harvesting   B.parafilm   C.epithelium   D.universal precautions

120. C   A method used by microbiologists and clinicians to keep cultures, sterile instruments and media, and people free of microbial contamination.
A.blood count   B.allergen   C.aseptic technique   D.nosocomial infection

121. D   Inflammation of a vein. The condition is marked by infiltration of the layers of the vein and the formation of a clot. It produces edema, stiffness and pain in the affected area.
A.blood cell   B.order of draw   C.antigen   D.phlebitis

122. B   Terminology used to define the order in which blood sample tubes should be drawn using a multi-sample technique such as the Vacutainer System.
A.blood   B.order of draw   C.bleeding time   D.engineering control

123. D   Used as a topical antiseptic, this is a compound made by reacting iodine with povidone which slowly releases iodine.
A.engineering control   B.fibrinogen   C.macrophage   D.povidone iodine

124. B   Pertaining to elements dissolved in blood or body fluids, e.g., homoral immunity from antibodies in the blood as opposed to cellular immunity.
A.vascular   B.humoral   C.venule   D.flexion

125. D   An implant or transplant of any tissue or organ.
A.hemoconcentration   B.cefibrinated blood   C.aspirate   D.graft

126. C   A type of coagulation (clotting) factors.
A.aseptic technique   B.bloodborne pathogens   C.antihemophilic factor   D.anesthetic

127. A   The upper or outer layer of the two main layers of cells that make up the skin.
A.epidermis   B.graft   C.aspirate   D.adsorb

128. A   The science concerned with the study of factors influencing the distribution of disease and their causes in a defined population.
A.epidemiology   B.hypersensitivity   C.heparin   D.macrophage

129. C   The hemoglobin compound bound with carbon dioxide in the red blood cells.
A.warfarin sodium   B.monocyte   C.carbamate hemoglobin   D.epidemiology

130. D   A preventative treatment.
A.adsorb   B.etiology   C.monocyte   D.prophylaxis

131. C   The swelling of soft tissues caused by excess fluid accumulation.
A.coagulation factors   B.pathogenic   C.edema   D.antiseptic

132. D   There are three main types of cell in the blood stream. The red cell, which carries oxygen, the white cell, which fights infections and the platelet, which helps prevent bleeding.
A.macrophage B.blood transfer device C.universal precautions D.blood cell

133. C   Called White Blood Cells. A variety of cells within the blood and bone marrow whose general purpose is to help in fighting infection.
A.cefibrinated blood B.macrophage C.leukocyte D.hemoconcentration

134. C   A technique in which blood products are separated from a donor and the desired elements collected and the rest returned to the donor.
A.etiology B.chelate C.apheresis D.faint

135. A   An abnormally low glucose level in the blood.
A.hypoglycemia B.venous C.harvesting D.parafilm

136. D   An agent that disinfects, applied particularly to agents used on inanimate objects.
A.aspirate B.blood culture C.absorb D.disinfectant

137. D   The number of red blood cells, white blood cells and platelets (per cubic millimeter) that are present in the patient's sample of blood is determined.
A.anemia B.epithelium C.distal D.complete blood count

138. C   A sudden loss of consciousness.
A.venous B.absorb C.faint D.flexion

139. C   A test which measures the time it takes for small blood vessels to close off and bleeding to stop.
A.mean corpuscular volume B.antigen C.bleeding time D.disinfectant

140. A   A safety device designed to transfer blood from one container into another.
A.blood transfer device B.blood C.coagulation factors D.fibrinogen

141. C   A test which involves the incubation of a blood specimen overnight to determine if bacteria are present.
A.proximal B.absorb C.blood culture D.carbamate hemoglobin

142. C   Of short duration. Rapid and abbreviated in onset.
A.thrombocytopenia B.proximal C.acute D.nosocomial infection

143. D   Pertaining to the veins, or blood passing through them.
A.hypodermic needle B.diaphoretic C.blood culture D.venous

144. A   The protein from which fibrin is formed.
A.fibrinogen B.allergen C.chromatin D.warfarin sodium

145. C   A process where polymorphonuclear leukocytes, monocytes, and macrophages combine with lysosomes within the cell cytoplasm to digest and destroy a particulate.
A.blood B.universal precautions C.phagocytosis D.vacutainer tube

146. B   Large vein on the inner side of the biceps. Often chosen for intravenous injections and blood drawing.
A.distal B.basilic vein C.collateral circulation D.epithelium

147. D   Having the capability of producing disease.
A.ecchymosis B.apheresis C.universal precautions D.pathogenic

148. B   White blood cells.
A.acute B.leukocyte C.antihemophilic factor D.circulation

149. B   Referring to the palm surface or side of the hand
   A.edema   B.palmar   C.cohorting   D.red blood cell

150. C   The membrane lining the abdominal and pelvic wall.
   A.pathogenic   B.engineering control   C.peritoneum   D.apheresis

151. A   A hospital-borne infection. An infection whose origin is from within the hospital environment.
   A.nosocomial infection   B.pathogen   C.epithelium   D.circulation

152. B   Blood sample tubes containing a vacuum. When the tube stopper is pierced by a Vacutainer
   needle which has been properly positioned in a vein, the vacuum draws blood into the tube.
   A.chelate   B.vacutainer tube   C.blood   D.antibody

153. C   As it relates to blood drawing, the material that is withdrawn with a negative pressure apparatus
   (syringe).
   A.diaphoretic   B.adsorb   C.aspirate   D.citrate phosphate dextrose

154. B   Something that discourages the growth microorganisms. By contrast, aseptic refers to the absence
   of microorganisms.
   A.vacutainer   B.antiseptic   C.thrombocyte   D.basal state

155. D   Formation of profuse perspiration (sweat). A symptom of syncope or vasovagal response.
   A.pathogenic   B.universal precautions   C.leukocyte   D.diaphoretic

156. D   The component of the blood that contains hemoglobin which is responsible for oxygen and carbon
   dioxide exchange.
   A.antihemophilic factor   B.pathogenic   C.epidemiology   D.red blood cell

157. A   Blood vessels carrying blood to the heart. Blood contained within these vessels is generally bound
   with carbon dioxide which will be exchanged for oxygen in the lungs.
   A.vein   B.allergen   C.red blood cell   D.basal state

158. C   To suck up, as through pores.
   A.hemoconcentration   B.anesthetic   C.absorb   D.leukocyte

159. A   Any microorganism that produces disease.
   A.pathogen   B.vacutainer   C.cefibrinated blood   D.basal state

160. C   A type of an arteriovenous fistula consisting of either a venous autograft or synthetic tube which is
   grafted to the artery and vein.
   A.hypersensitivity   B.peritoneum   C.vascular graft   D.diaphoretic

161. B   Precautions that are designed for the care of all patients in hospitals regardless of their diagnosis
   or presumed infection status.
   A.cohorting   B.standard precautions   C.hemolysis   D.flexion

162. D   An anticoagulant.
   A.vascular graft   B.vacutainer   C.flexion   D.citrate phosphate dextrose

163. B   The more readily stainable portion of the cell nucleus. It is a DNA attached to a protein structure
   and is the carrier of genes in inheritance.
   A.macrophage   B.chromatin   C.hypodermic needle   D.basilic vein

164. C   Average volume of red blood cells.
   A.apheresis   B.complete blood count   C.mean corpuscular volume   D.venous

165. D   Remote, farther from any point of reference, opposed to proximal
   A.heparin   B.contamination   C.collateral circulation   D.distal

166. C The breaking of the red blood cells membrane releasing free hemoglobin into the circulating blood.
A.epidemiology B.prophylaxis C.hemolysis D.vacutainer tube

167. A Combining with a metallic ion into a ring complex.
A.chelate B.thrombus C.blood group D.edema

168. B To examine or feel by the hand. In relation to venipunctures, this technique is used to "feel" a vein which will tend to rebound when slight pressure is applied with the finger.
A.monocyte B.palpate C.antiseptic D.differential

169. D Pertaining to or composed of blood vessels. The vascular system is composed of the heart, blood vessels, lymphatics and their parts considered collectively.
A.vacutainer tube B.differential C.antihemophilic factor D.vascular

170. C Decrease in the number of blood platelets below normal values.
A.allergen B.povidone iodine C.thrombocytopenia D.blood group

171. C Controls (e.g., sharps disposal containers, self-sheathing needles) that isolate or remove the bloodborne pathogens hazard from the workplace.
A.vascular graft B.edema C.engineering control D.leukocyte

172. A An abnormal passageway usually between two internal organs. Such passages may be created experimentally for obtaining body secretions for study.
A.fistula B.palmar C.blood vessel D.antigen

173. C An object or material, such as tissue, partially or totally inserted or grafted into the body of a recipient.
A.antigen B.citrate phosphate dextrose C.implant D.parafilm

174. B The cause or origin of a disease or disorder.
A.heparin B.etiology C.nosocomial infection D.ecchymosis

175. B A needle that attaches to a syringe for injections or withdrawal of fluids such as blood.
A.harvesting B.hypodermic needle C.aseptic technique D.phlebitis

176. D The movement of fluid in a regular or circuitous course.
A.disinfectant B.blood culture C.collateral circulation D.circulation

177. A A count made on a stained blood smear of the proportion of the different leukocytes (WBC's) and expressed as a percentage.
A.differential B.heparin C.absorb D.edema

178. B The oxygen carrying pigment of the red blood cells.
A.circulation B.hemoglobin C.red blood cell D.distal

179. C A substance capable of producing a specific immune response with a specific antibody.
A.allergen B.hemolysis C.antigen D.coagulation factors

180. D A blood clot obstructing a blood vessel or a cavity of the heart. Heparin and Warfarin Sodium are being used to assist in dissolving or preventing clot formations.
A.red blood cell B.nosocomial infection C.anemia D.thrombus

181. B Nearest to any other point of reference.
A.standard precautions B.proximal C.absorb D.apheresis

182. C Blood which has been deprived of fibrin.
A.contamination B.cohorting C.cefibrinated blood D.blood group

183. C   The state of the body early in the morning, approximately 12 hours after the last ingestion of food or other nutrition.
    A.order of draw   B.palmar   C.basal state   D.monocyte

184. C   The collection and preservation of tissues or cells from a donor for transplantation.
    A.chelate   B.antihemophilic factor   C.harvesting   D.implant

185. A   An inherited feature on the surface of the red blood cell. A series of related blood groups make up a blood group system such as the ABO system or the Rh system.
    A.blood group   B.harvesting   C.thrombus   D.bloodborne pathogens

186. D   To attract and retain other material on the surface.
    A.thrombocytopenia   B.red blood cell   C.fistula   D.adsorb

187. B   A trade name now a generic term used to describe equipment used to automatically aspirate blood from a vessel by venipuncture.
    A.thrombus   B.vacutainer   C.universal precautions   D.monocyte

188. A   The skin discoloration caused by a bruise (contusion).
    A.ecchymosis   B.diaphoretic   C.venule   D.hemolysis

189. A   Group of plasma protein substances (Factor I thru XIII) contained in the plasma, which act together to bring about blood coagulation.
    A.coagulation factors   B.hemoglobin   C.blood count   D.red blood cell

190. A   A hardening, especially from inflammation and certain disease states. Though sclerosis may occur in many areas of the body, the term is most often associated with blood vessels.
    A.sclerosis   B.citrate phosphate dextrose   C.vascular graft   D.leukocyte

191. C   A mononuclear, phagocytic leukocyte.
    A.nosocomial infection   B.carbamate hemoglobin   C.monocyte   D.palmar

192. B   The formation of a blood clot (thrombus) within a vessel.
    A.blood culture   B.thrombosis   C.antiseptic   D.bloodborne pathogens

193. A   Any disease producing microorganism which is spread through direct contact with contaminated blood.
    A.bloodborne pathogens   B.cefibrinated blood   C.blood   D.complete blood count

194. D   The sodium salt of warfarin, one of the synthetic anticoagulants. Coumadin is a brand name.
    A.ecchymosis   B.macrophage   C.absorb   D.warfarin sodium

195. A   A state in which the body reacts with an exaggerated immune response to a foreign substance. Reactions are classified as delayed or immediate types.
    A.hypersensitivity   B.antigen   C.absorb   D.blood cell

196. C   The determination of the proper number of red blood cells, white blood cells and platelets are present in the patient's blood.
    A.sclerosis   B.blood group   C.blood count   D.harvesting

197. B   Blood which infuses an area through a secondary or accessory route.
    A.cefibrinated blood   B.collateral circulation   C.apheresis   D.basilic vein

198. C   Situated at the back (dorsal) part of a structure.
    A.blood cell   B.proximal   C.posterior   D.phagocytosis

199. B   A large vein of the arm that empties into the axillary vein
    A.gauge   B.cephalic vein   C.fibrinogen   D.acute

200. B   A drug that causes unconsciousness or a loss of general sensation. A local anesthetic causes loss of feeling in a part of the body.
A.aseptic technique   B.anesthetic   C.leukocyte   D.epidermis

From the words provided for each clue, provide the letter of the word which best matches the clue.

201. D   The surgical joining of an artery and a vein under the skin for hemodialysis.
A.fasting   B.supine   C.engineering control   D.arteriovenous fistula

202. C   Fluid found in lymphatic vessels and nodes derived from tissue fluids. Lymph is collected from all parts of the body and returned to the blood by the lymphatic system.
A.fasting   B.syncope   C.lymph   D.vacutainer holder

203. D   Also known as a platelet, this is a particulate component of the blood, approximately 2-4 microns in diameter and known for its involvement in blood coagulation.
A.arteriovenous fistula   B.hemoconcentration   C.faint   D.thrombocyte

204. C   The cause or origin of a disease or disorder.
A.pathogenic   B.heparin   C.etiology   D.vacutainer holder

205. C   Fainting; a temporary loss of consciousness due to a reduction of blood to the brain.
A.vacutainer holder   B.lymph   C.syncope   D.engineering control

206. C   Having the capability of producing disease.
A.lymph   B.hemoconcentration   C.pathogenic   D.contagious

207. A   There are three main types of cell in the blood stream. The red cell, which carries oxygen, the white cell, which fights infections and the platelet, which helps prevent bleeding.
A.blood cell   B.pathogenic   C.engineering control   D.supine

208. A   Infectious. May be transmitted from person to person.
A.contagious   B.lymph   C.thrombocyte   D.blood cell

209. A   Lying down with the face up; opposed to prone.
A.supine   B.hemoconcentration   C.vacutainer holder   D.fasting

210. C   Without eating. Some laboratory tests are performed on "fasting" blood specimens such as sugar (glucose) levels and tolerance tests such as glucose, lactose and dextrose.
A.thrombocyte   B.pathogenic   C.fasting   D.vacutainer holder

211. B   An anticoagulant that acts to inhibit coagulation factors, especially factor Xa. Heparin is formed in the liver.
A.lymph   B.heparin   C.etiology   D.thrombocyte

212. C   A cylindrical shaped holder that accepts a Vacutainer tube on one end and a Vacutainer needle on the other.
A.lymph   B.etiology   C.vacutainer holder   D.thrombocyte

213. B   A decrease in the fluid content of the blood (plasma), resulting in an increase in concentration. This is determined by an increase in the hematocrit. Caused by a filtration of plasma into body tissues and often created by dehydration.
A.pathogenic   B.hemoconcentration   C.faint   D.blood cell

214. D   Controls (e.g., sharps disposal containers, self-sheathing needles) that isolate or remove the bloodborne pathogens hazard from the workplace.
A.supine   B.lymph   C.arteriovenous fistula   D.engineering control

215. B A sudden loss of consciousness.
A.fasting B.faint C.contagious D.pathogenic

Matching

Provide the word that best matches each clue.

1. _____ The incision of a vein as for blood-letting (venesection); needle puncture of a vein for drawing blood (venipuncture).

2. _____ Without eating. Some laboratory tests are performed on "fasting" blood specimens such as sugar (glucose) levels and tolerance tests such as glucose, lactose and dextrose.

3. _____ A sample of blood is applied to a microscope slide and then studied under the microscope.

4. _____ A position farther from the midline of the body or another reference structure.

5. _____ Lying face down; opposed to supine.

6. _____ Combining with a metallic ion into a ring complex.

7. _____ Fluid found in lymphatic vessels and nodes derived from tissue fluids. Lymph is collected from all parts of the body and returned to the blood by the lymphatic system.

8. _____ A sudden loss of consciousness.

9. _____ The surgical joining of an artery and a vein under the skin for hemodialysis.

10. _____ The outside layer of cells that covers all the free, open surfaces of the body including the skin, and mucous membranes that communicate with the outside of the body.

11. _____ That part of the arm opposing the elbow.

12. _____ The fluid in the body that contains red cells and white cells as well as platelets, proteins, plasma and other elements. It is transported throughout the body by the Circulatory System.

13. _____ A blood clot obstructing a blood vessel or a cavity of the heart. Heparin and Warfarin Sodium are being used to assist in dissolving or preventing clot formations.

14. _____ Situated at the back (dorsal) part of a structure.

15. _____ An anticoagulant.

16. _____ Toward the front or in front of.

17. _____ An eosin (red) staining leukocyte with a nucleus that usually has two lobes connected by a slender thread of chromatin, and cytoplasm containing coarse, round granules that are uniform in size.

18. _____ Pertaining to the front side of the body.

19. _____ To attract and retain other material on the surface.

20. _____ Main protein in human blood.

21. _____ The upper or outer layer of the two main layers of cells that make up the skin.

22. _____ The viscid, translucent fluid that makes up the essential material of all plant and animal cells.

23. _____ A decrease in the fluid content of the blood (plasma), resulting in an increase in concentration. This is determined by an increase in the hematocrit. Caused by a filtration of plasma into body tissues and often created by dehydration.

24. _____ In epidemiology, a group of individuals who share common characteristics.

25. _____ The oxygen carrying pigment of the red blood cells.

26. _____ An object or material, such as tissue, partially or totally inserted or grafted into the body of a recipient.

A. Protoplasm	B. Ventral	C. Blood
D. Lateral	E. Prone	F. Lymph
G. Phlebotomy	H. Faint	I. Epidermis
J. Adsorb	K. Arteriovenous fistula	L. Albumin
M. Chelate	N. Thrombus	O. Cohorting
P. Blood film	Q. Citrate phosphate dextrose	R. Fasting
S. Posterior	T. Hemoglobin	U. Anterior
V. Implant	W. Epithelium	X. Eosinophil
Y. Hemoconcentration	Z. Antecubital fossa	

Provide the word that best matches each clue.

27. _____ Human Immunodeficiency Virus

28. _____ A small pointed blade usually with two edges used for incising or puncturing.

29. _____ Pertaining to results obtained through treatment; having medicinal or healing properties; a healing agent.

30. _____ Enclosed containers used to hold specimen tubes for centrifugation.

31. _____ The determination of the proper number of red blood cells, white blood cells and platelets are present in the patient's blood.

32. _____ A cylindrical shaped holder that accepts a Vacutainer tube on one end and a Vacutainer needle on the other.

33. _____ Growing, living or occurring in the absence of molecular oxygen; pertaining to an anaerobe.

34. _____ Lying face down; opposed to supine.

35. _____ Without eating. Some laboratory tests are performed on "fasting" blood specimens such as sugar (glucose) levels and tolerance tests such as glucose, lactose and dextrose.

36. _____ Referring to collection of blood specimens by puncturing capillaries, usually in the heel of infants or the fingers of children and adults.

37. _____ Dialysis through the peritoneum.

38. _____ The hemoglobin compound bound with carbon dioxide in the red blood cells.

39. _____ The absence of microorganisms. By contrast, something that just discourages the growth of microorganisms is antiseptic.

40. _____ A hardening, especially from inflammation and certain disease states. Though sclerosis may occur in many areas of the body, the term is most often associated with blood vessels.

41. _____ The cause or origin of a disease or disorder.

42. _____ Medications that, like aspirin, reduce the tendency of platelets in the blood to clump and clot.

43. _____ Inflammation of a vein. The condition is marked by infiltration of the layers of the vein and the formation of a clot. It produces edema, stiffness and pain in the affected area.

44. _____ The ratio of the total red blood cell volume to the total blood volume and expressed as a percentage.

45. _____ Pertaining to elements dissolved in blood or body fluids, e.g., homoral immunity from antibodies in the blood as opposed to cellular immunity.

46. _____ A laboratory apparatus that separates mixed samples into homogenous component layers by spinning them at high speed.

47. _____ The component of the blood that contains hemoglobin which is responsible for oxygen and carbon dioxide exchange.

48. _____ Fainting; a temporary loss of consciousness due to a reduction of blood to the brain.

49. _____ Abbreviation for the Latin word statim, meaning immediately.

50. _____ A semisolid mass of blood found inside or outside the body.

51. _____ A glass or transparent plastic tube used to accurately measure small amounts of liquid.

52. _____ A thin film of paraffin used primarily in the laboratory to seal open containers such as test tubes.

A. Aseptic
D. Antiplatelet agent
G. Blood count
J. Therapeutic
M. Parafilm
P. Etiology
S. Pipet
V. Phlebitis
Y. Syncope

B. Sclerosis
E. Microcapillary
H. Aerosol canisters
K. Lancet
N. Red blood cell
Q. Hematocrit
T. Fasting
W. Vacutainer Holder
Z. Humoral

C. Carbamate hemoglobin
F. Centrifuge
I. HIV
L. Peritoneal dialysis
O. Anaerobic
R. Stat
U. Prone
X. Clot

Provide the word that best matches each clue.

53. _____ A process where polymorphonuclear leukocytes, monocytes, and macrophages combine with lysosomes within the cell cytoplasm to digest and destroy a particulate.

54. _____ Pertaining to elements dissolved in blood or body fluids, e.g., homoral immunity from antibodies in the blood as opposed to cellular immunity.

55. _____ White blood cells.

56. _____ A constrictive band, placed over an extremity to distend veins for blood aspiration or intravenous injections.

57. _____ Also known as a thrombocyte, this is a particulate component of the blood known for its involvement in blood coagulation.

58. _____ A technique in which blood products are separated from a donor and the desired elements collected and the rest returned to the donor.

59. _____ As it relates to blood drawing, the material that is withdrawn with a negative pressure apparatus (syringe).

60. _____ A test which involves the incubation of a blood specimen overnight to determine if bacteria are present.

61. _____ Blood vessels carrying blood to the heart. Blood contained within these vessels is generally bound with carbon dioxide which will be exchanged for oxygen in the lungs.

62. _____ The movement of fluid in a regular or circuitous course.

63. _____ A substance that will acquire the capacity to conduct electricity when put into solution. Electrolytes include sodium, potassium, chloride, calcium and phosphate.

64. _____ Blood from which none of the elements have been removed.

65. _____ A thin film of paraffin used primarily in the laboratory to seal open containers such as test tubes.

66. _____ Blood vessel carrying blood away from the heart. Arterial blood is normally full of oxygen.

67. _____ The hemoglobin compound bound with carbon dioxide in the red blood cells.

68. _____ An abnormally low glucose level in the blood.

69. _____ Average volume of red blood cells.

70. _____ To suck up, as through pores.

71. _____ The sugar measured in blood and urine specimens to determine the presence or absence of diabetes. Glucose is the product of carbohydrate metabolism and is the chief source of energy for all living organisms.

72. _____ A substance that will acquire the capacity to conduct electricity when put into solution.

73. _____ The liquid portion of a cell including organelles and inclusions suspended in it. It is the site of most chemical activities of the cell.

74. _____ Fainting; a temporary loss of consciousness due to a reduction of blood to the brain.

75. _____ Any small space of cavity formed in the protoplasm of a cell.

76. _____ The process of clot formation. Part of an important host defense mechanism call hemostasis.

77. _____ A mononuclear, phagocytic leukocyte.

78. _____ Toward the front or in front of.

A. Tourniquet	B. Cytoplasm	C. Parafilm
D. Anterior	E. Vein	F. Platelet
G. Humoral	H. Circulation	I. Electrolyte
J. Vacuole	K. Lytes	L. Absorb
M. Aspirate	N. Mean Corpuscular Volume	O. Glucose
P. Coagulate	Q. Carbamate hemoglobin	R. Monocyte
S. Hypoglycemia	T. Leukocyte	U. Syncope
V. Phagocytosis	W. Blood culture	X. Whole blood
Y. Apheresis	Z. Artery	

Provide the word that best matches each clue.

79. _____ An anticoagulant.

80. _____ The protein from which fibrin is formed.

81. _____ The cessation of bleeding, either by vasoconstriction and coagulation or by surgical means.

82. _____ Medications that, like aspirin, reduce the tendency of platelets in the blood to clump and clot.

83. _____ The breaking of the red blood cells membrane releasing free hemoglobin into the circulating blood.

84. _____ The number of white blood cells (leukocytes) found in the peripheral blood and measured per cubic millimeter.

85. _____ A type of coagulation (clotting) factors.

86. _____ A very tiny vein, continuous with the capillaries. Compare with arteriole.

87. _____ A test which involves the incubation of a blood specimen overnight to determine if bacteria are present.

88. _____ Fainting; a temporary loss of consciousness due to a reduction of blood to the brain.

89. _____ Outside the living body; inside a glass; observable in a test tube.

90. _____ Blood vessel carrying blood away from the heart. Arterial blood is normally full of oxygen.

91. _____ The circulatory system is composed of the heart, arteries, capillaries and veins.

92. _____ The movement of fluid in a regular or circuitous course.

93. _____ Denoting a position more toward the back surface than some other object of reference; same as posterior in human anatomy.

94. _____ A group or series of enzymatic reactions in living aerobic organisms that results in the production of energy.

95. _____ The conversion of blood from a liquid form to solid through the process of coagulation.

96. _____ An object or material, such as tissue, partially or totally inserted or grafted into the body of a recipient.

97. _____ The presence of viable bacteria circulating in the bloodstream. Diagnosed with blood cultures.

98. _____ Blood which infuses an area through a secondary or accessory route.

99. _____ Pertaining to the front side of the body.

100. _____ The outside layer of cells that covers all the free, open surfaces of the body including the skin, and mucous membranes that communicate with the outside of the body.

101. _____ An acute, generalized life-threatening allergic or hypersensitive reaction.

102. _____ Inflammation of the liver.

103. _____ Nearest to any other point of reference.

104. _____ An abnormal passageway usually between two internal organs. Such passages may be created experimentally for obtaining body secretions for study.

A. Syncope	B. Citrate phosphate dextrose	C. Anaphylaxis
D. Epithelium	E. White blood cell count	F. Fistula
G. Ventral	H. Antihemophilic factor	I. Hemostasis
J. Circulatory System	K. Artery	L. Bacteremia
M. Citric Acid Cycle	N. Blood clot	O. Invitro
P. Implant	Q. Collateral circulation	R. Proximal
S. Antiplatelet agent	T. Venule	U. Circulation
V. Dorsal	W. Hepatitis	X. Hemolysis
Y. Fibrinogen	Z. Blood culture	

Provide the word that best matches each clue.

105. _____ A preventative treatment.

106. _____ A test which measures the time it takes for small blood vessels to close off and bleeding to stop.

107. _____ Blood vessels carrying blood to the heart. Blood contained within these vessels is generally bound with carbon dioxide which will be exchanged for oxygen in the lungs.

108. _____ Inside the living body.

109. _____ Any of the many forms of mononuclear phagocytes found in tissues and originating from stem cells in the bone marrow. In normal circulation, the monocyte may be categorized as a macrophage.

110. _____ A hardening, especially from inflammation and certain disease states. Though sclerosis may occur in many areas of the body, the term is most often associated with blood vessels.

111. _____ Usually a self-limited viral disease. Transmission is usually the result of poor hygiene and most often through the fecal-oral route.

112. _____ Pertaining to the middle aspect; closer to the midline of the body or structure.

113. _____ The most common form of hepatitis after blood transfusion. It is also the most prevalent form resulting from needle sharing by drug abusers.

114. _____ The surgical joining of an artery and a vein under the skin for hemodialysis.

115. _____ Relative to venipunctures, the appearance of a small amount of blood in the neck of a syringe or the tubing of a butterfly. This is a sign that the vein has been properly accessed.

116. _____ A bruise or ""contusion" is a traumatic injury of the soft tissues which results in breakage of the local capillaries and leakage of red blood cells.

117. _____ A thin film of paraffin used primarily in the laboratory to seal open containers such as test tubes.

118. _____ The fluid in the body that contains red cells and white cells as well as platelets, proteins, plasma and other elements. It is transported throughout the body by the Circulatory System.

119. _____ A needle that attaches to a syringe for injections or withdrawal of fluids such as blood.

120. _____ A calcium chelating (binding) agent that is used as an anticoagulant for laboratory blood specimens. Also used in treatment of lead poisoning.

121. _____ Fluid found in lymphatic vessels and nodes derived from tissue fluids. Lymph is collected from all parts of the body and returned to the blood by the lymphatic system.

122. _____ Decrease in the number of blood platelets below normal values.

123. _____ A laboratory apparatus that separates mixed samples into homogenous component layers by spinning them at high speed.

124. _____ A process where polymorphonuclear leukocytes, monocytes, and macrophages combine with lysosomes within the cell cytoplasm to digest and destroy a particulate.

125. _____ The hemoglobin compound bound with carbon dioxide in the red blood cells.

126. _____ Inflammation of the liver.

127. _____ An implant or transplant of any tissue or organ.

128. _____ Any different protein factors which, when acting together, can form a blood clot shortly after platelets have broken at the site of the wound.

129. _____ Pertaining to elements dissolved in blood or body fluids, e.g., homoral immunity from antibodies in the blood as opposed to cellular immunity.

130. _____ Formation of profuse perspiration (sweat). A symptom of syncope or vasovagal response.

A. Thrombocytopenia
B. Parafilm
C. EDTA
D. Medial
E. Macrophage
F. Blood
G. Blood clotting factor
H. Graft
I. Diaphoretic
J. Hypodermic needle
K. Hepatitis
L. Flash back
M. Sclerosis
N. Hepatitis C
O. Hepatitis A
P. Carbamate hemoglobin
Q. Invivo
R. Centrifuge
S. Phagocytosis
T. Bleeding time
U. Bruise
V. Humoral
W. Lymph
X. Arteriovenous fistula
Y. Vein
Z. Prophylaxis

Provide the word that best matches each clue.

131. _____ Any small space of cavity formed in the protoplasm of a cell.

132. _____ A hardening, especially from inflammation and certain disease states. Though sclerosis may occur in many areas of the body, the term is most often associated with blood vessels.

133. _____ The science concerned with the study of factors influencing the distribution of disease and their causes in a defined population.

134. _____ A trade name now a generic term used to describe equipment used to automatically aspirate blood from a vessel by venipuncture.

135. _____ A state in which the body reacts with an exaggerated immune response to a foreign substance. Reactions are classified as delayed or immediate types.

136. _____ Also known as a platelet, this is a particulate component of the blood, approximately 2-4 microns in diameter and known for its involvement in blood coagulation.

137. _____ A group or series of enzymatic reactions in living aerobic organisms that results in the production of energy.

138. _____ To suck up, as through pores.

139. _____ An abnormally low glucose level in the blood.

140. _____ The hemoglobin compound bound with carbon dioxide in the red blood cells.

141. _____ Pertaining to the front side of the body.

142. _____ Precautions that are designed for the care of all patients in hospitals regardless of their diagnosis or presumed infection status.

143. _____ Fainting; a temporary loss of consciousness due to a reduction of blood to the brain.

144. _____ To attract and retain other material on the surface.

145. _____ The conversion of blood from a liquid form to solid through the process of coagulation.

146. _____ A type of an arteriovenous fistula consisting of either a venous autograft or synthetic tube which is grafted to the artery and vein.

147. _____ A large vein of the arm that empties into the axillary vein

148. _____ To examine or feel by the hand. In relation to venipunctures, this technique is used to "feel" a vein which will tend to rebound when slight pressure is applied with the finger.

149. _____ An acute form of hepatitis caused by a virus. The virus is shed in body fluids of chronic and acute patients as well as asymptomatic carriers.

150. _____ Inside the living body.

151. _____ Cells that carry oxygen to all parts of the body.

152. _____ A constrictive band, placed over an extremity to distend veins for blood aspiration or intravenous injections.

153. _____ The process of clot formation. Part of an important host defense mechanism call hemostasis.

154. _____ The protein from which fibrin is formed.

155. _____ Main protein in human blood.

156. _____ Any of the many forms of mononuclear phagocytes found in tissues and originating from stem cells in the bone marrow. In normal circulation, the monocyte may be categorized as a macrophage.

A. Blood clot
D. Hypoglycemia
G. Standard Precautions
J. Vascular graft
M. Cephalic vein
P. Absorb
S. Ventral
V. Hepatitis B
Y. Citric Acid Cycle

B. Hypersensitivity
E. Vacuole
H. Erythrocyte
K. Carbamate hemoglobin
N. Albumin
Q. Syncope
T. Sclerosis
W. Invivo
Z. Epidemiology

C. Fibrinogen
F. Palpate
I. Macrophage
L. Thrombocyte
O. Vacutainer
R. Coagulate
U. Adsorb
X. Tourniquet

Provide the word that best matches each clue.

157. _____ Fainting; a temporary loss of consciousness due to a reduction of blood to the brain.

158. _____ A tube for insertion into a duct or cavity.

159. _____ The number of red blood cells, white blood cells and platelets (per cubic millimeter) that are present in the patient's sample of blood is determined.

160. _____ Enclosed containers used to hold specimen tubes for centrifugation.

161. _____ An acute form of hepatitis caused by a virus. The virus is shed in body fluids of chronic and acute patients as well as asymptomatic carriers.

162. _____ Dialysis through the peritoneum.

163. _____ The protein formed during normal blood clotting that is the essence of the clot.

164. _____ Blood vessel carrying blood away from the heart. Arterial blood is normally full of oxygen.

165. _____ Paleness; decrease of absence of skin color.

166. _____ An organ or tissue taken from the body for grafting into another part of the same body or into another individual.

167. _____ The liquid portion of a cell including organelles and inclusions suspended in it. It is the site of most chemical activities of the cell.

168. _____ The hemoglobin compound bound with carbon dioxide in the red blood cells.

169. _____ The condition of having less than the normal number of red blood cells or hemoglobin in the blood.

170. _____ The determination of the proper number of red blood cells, white blood cells and platelets are present in the patient's blood.

171. _____ A type of swelling which occurs in lymphatic tissue when excess fluid collects in the arms or legs because the lymph nodes or vessels are blocked or removed.

172. _____ The soiling by inferior material, as by the introduction of organisms into a wound.

173. _____ The circulatory system is composed of the heart, arteries, capillaries and veins.

174. _____ A count made on a stained blood smear of the proportion of the different leukocytes (WBC's) and expressed as a percentage.

175. _____ Of short duration. Rapid and abbreviated in onset.

176. _____ Performing a venipuncture with no apparently visible or palpable vein.

177. _____ One who practices phlebotomy.

178. _____ Pertaining to results obtained through treatment; having medicinal or healing properties; a healing agent.

179. _____ The skin discoloration caused by a bruise (contusion).

180. _____ As it relates to blood drawing, the material that is withdrawn with a negative pressure apparatus (syringe).

181. _____ A hardening, especially from inflammation and certain disease states. Though sclerosis may occur in many areas of the body, the term is most often associated with blood vessels.

182. _____ To attract and retain other material on the surface.

A. Ecchymosis   B. Syncope   C. Blind stick
D. Therapeutic   E. Adsorb   F. Carbamate hemoglobin

G. Cannula
J. Cytoplasm
M. Complete blood count
P. Artery
S. Phlebotomist
V. Blood count
Y. Transplant

H. Pallor
K. Lymphedema
N. Aspirate
Q. Peritoneal dialysis
T. Aerosol canisters
W. Differential
Z. Acute

I. Anemia
L. Circulatory System
O. Sclerosis
R. Contamination
U. Fibrin
X. Hepatitis B

Provide the word that best matches each clue.

183. _____ White blood cells.

184. _____ The ratio of the total red blood cell volume to the total blood volume and expressed as a percentage.

185. _____ A needle that attaches to a syringe for injections or withdrawal of fluids such as blood.

186. _____ A hospital-borne infection. An infection whose origin is from within the hospital environment.

187. _____ A mononuclear, phagocytic leukocyte.

188. _____ A laboratory apparatus that separates mixed samples into homogenous component layers by spinning them at high speed.

189. _____ Blood vessels carrying blood to the heart. Blood contained within these vessels is generally bound with carbon dioxide which will be exchanged for oxygen in the lungs.

190. _____ The determination of the proper number of red blood cells, white blood cells and platelets are present in the patient's blood.

191. _____ Having the capability of producing disease.

192. _____ This precaution is for specified patients known or suspected to be infected or colonized with microorganisms that can be transmitted by direct contact with the patient.

193. _____ Inflammation of the liver.

194. _____ Remote, farther from any point of reference, opposed to proximal

195. _____ A decrease in the inside diameter of especially arterioles leading to a decrease in blood flow to a part.

196. _____ Pertaining to or composed of blood vessels. The vascular system is composed of the heart, blood vessels, lymphatics and their parts considered collectively.

197. _____ Pertaining to the front side of the body.

198. _____ To examine or feel by the hand. In relation to venipunctures, this technique is used to "feel" a vein which will tend to rebound when slight pressure is applied with the finger.

199. _____ A blood clot obstructing a blood vessel or a cavity of the heart. Heparin and Warfarin Sodium are being used to assist in dissolving or preventing clot formations.

200. _____ An antigenic substance capable of producing an immediate-type hypersensitivity (allergy).

201. _____ Inflammation of a vein. The condition is marked by infiltration of the layers of the vein and the formation of a clot. It produces edema, stiffness and pain in the affected area.

202. _____ The puncture of a vein for any purpose

203. _____ A test which measures the time it takes for small blood vessels to close off and bleeding to stop.

204. _____ Lying down with the face up; opposed to prone.

205. _____ A technique in which blood products are separated from a donor and the desired elements collected and the rest returned to the donor.

206. _____ A localized collection of blood within tissue due to leakage from the wall of a blood vessel, producing a bluish discoloration (ecchymosis)and pain.

207. _____ Main protein in human blood.

208. _____ A sudden loss of consciousness.

A. Vasoconstriction
B. Pathogenic
C. Centrifuge
D. Supine
E. Contact Precautions
F. Palpate
G. Nosocomial infection
H. Faint
I. Hepatitis
J. Vein
K. Apheresis
L. Distal
M. Bleeding time
N. Thrombus
O. Blood count
P. Hematoma
Q. Albumin
R. Venipuncture
S. Allergen
T. Phlebitis
U. Monocyte
V. Ventral
W. Hypodermic needle
X. Hematocrit
Y. Leukocyte
Z. Vascular

Provide the word that best matches each clue.

209. _____ An isolation procedure designed to protect the patient from contracting disease. Frequently used for transplant patients or for patients whose immune response has been greatly reduced.

210. _____ A sample of blood is applied to a microscope slide and then studied under the microscope.

211. _____ Precautions that are designed for the care of all patients in hospitals regardless of their diagnosis or presumed infection status.

212. _____ The sodium salt of warfarin, one of the synthetic anticoagulants. Coumadin is a brand name.

213. _____ A hardening, especially from inflammation and certain disease states. Though sclerosis may occur in many areas of the body, the term is most often associated with blood vessels.

214. _____ A decrease in the inside diameter of especially arterioles leading to a decrease in blood flow to a part.

215. _____ Inflammation of the liver.

216. _____ To attract and retain other material on the surface.

217. _____ A semisolid mass of blood found inside or outside the body.

218. _____ The swelling of soft tissues caused by excess fluid accumulation.

219. _____ A safety device designed to transfer blood from one container into another.

220. _____ A transient vascular and neurogenic reaction marked by pallor, nausea, sweating, slowing heart rate and a rapid fall in arterial blood pressure which may result in loss of consciousness.

221. _____ A brand name for warfarin sodium.

222. _____ The absence of microorganisms. By contrast, something that just discourages the growth of microorganisms is antiseptic.

223. _____ Paleness; decrease of absence of skin color.

224. _____ The selective separation and removal of platelets from withdrawn blood. The remainder of the blood is re-transfused back into the donor.

225. _____ The component of the blood that contains hemoglobin which is responsible for oxygen and carbon dioxide exchange.

226. _____ Called White Blood Cells. A variety of cells within the blood and bone marrow whose general purpose is to help in fighting infection.

227. _____ The process of bending or the state of being bent. Flexion of the fingers results in a clenched fist.

228. _____ Toward the front or in front of.

229. _____ Combining with a metallic ion into a ring complex.

230. _____ An acute, generalized life-threatening allergic or hypersensitive reaction.

231. _____ A large vein of the arm that empties into the axillary vein

232. _____ This precaution is for specified patients known or suspected to be infected or colonized with microorganisms that can be transmitted by direct contact with the patient.

233. _____ A position farther from the midline of the body or another reference structure.

234. _____ The forearm vein most commonly used for venipuncture because it is generally the largest and best-anchored vein

A. Anterior	B. Leukocyte	C. Aseptic	D. Anaphylaxis
E. Standard Precautions	F. Reverse isolation	G. Pallor	H. Blood film
I. Vasovagal response	J. Plateletpheresis	K. Flexion	L. Medial cubital vein
M. Coumadin	N. Chelate	O. Adsorb	P. Sclerosis
Q. Edema	R. Hepatitis	S. Blood transfer device	T. Cephalic vein
U. Clot	V. Red blood cell	W. Lateral	X. Vasoconstriction
Y. Contact Precautions	Z. Warfarin sodium		

Provide the word that best matches each clue.

1. PHLEBOTOMY — The incision of a vein as for blood-letting (venesection); needle puncture of a vein for drawing blood (venipuncture).

2. FASTING — Without eating. Some laboratory tests are performed on "fasting" blood specimens such as sugar (glucose) levels and tolerance tests such as glucose, lactose and dextrose.

3. BLOOD FILM — A sample of blood is applied to a microscope slide and then studied under the microscope.

4. LATERAL — A position farther from the midline of the body or another reference structure.

5. PRONE — Lying face down; opposed to supine.

6. CHELATE — Combining with a metallic ion into a ring complex.

7. LYMPH — Fluid found in lymphatic vessels and nodes derived from tissue fluids. Lymph is collected from all parts of the body and returned to the blood by the lymphatic system.

8. FAINT — A sudden loss of consciousness.

9. ARTERIOVENOUS FISTULA — The surgical joining of an artery and a vein under the skin for hemodialysis.

10. EPITHELIUM — The outside layer of cells that covers all the free, open surfaces of the body including the skin, and mucous membranes that communicate with the outside of the body.

11. ANTECUBITAL FOSSA — That part of the arm opposing the elbow.

12. BLOOD — The fluid in the body that contains red cells and white cells as well as platelets, proteins, plasma and other elements. It is transported throughout the body by the Circulatory System.

13. THROMBUS — A blood clot obstructing a blood vessel or a cavity of the heart. Heparin and Warfarin Sodium are being used to assist in dissolving or preventing clot formations.

14. POSTERIOR — Situated at the back (dorsal) part of a structure.

15. CITRATE PHOSPHATE DEXTROSE — An anticoagulant.

16. ANTERIOR _____ Toward the front or in front of.

17. EOSINOPHIL _____ An eosin (red) staining leukocyte with a nucleus that usually has two lobes connected by a slender thread of chromatin, and cytoplasm containing coarse, round granules that are uniform in size.

18. VENTRAL _____ Pertaining to the front side of the body.

19. ADSORB _____ To attract and retain other material on the surface.

20. ALBUMIN _____ Main protein in human blood.

21. EPIDERMIS _____ The upper or outer layer of the two main layers of cells that make up the skin.

22. PROTOPLASM _____ The viscid, translucent fluid that makes up the essential material of all plant and animal cells.

23. HEMOCONCENTRATION _____ A decrease in the fluid content of the blood (plasma), resulting in an increase in concentration. This is determined by an increase in the hematocrit. Caused by a filtration of plasma into body tissues and often created by dehydration.

24. COHORTING _____ In epidemiology, a group of individuals who share common characteristics.

25. HEMOGLOBIN _____ The oxygen carrying pigment of the red blood cells.

26. IMPLANT _____ An object or material, such as tissue, partially or totally inserted or grafted into the body of a recipient.

A. Protoplasm	B. Ventral	C. Blood
D. Lateral	E. Prone	F. Lymph
G. Phlebotomy	H. Faint	I. Epidermis
J. Adsorb	K. Arteriovenous fistula	L. Albumin
M. Chelate	N. Thrombus	O. Cohorting
P. Blood film	Q. Citrate phosphate dextrose	R. Fasting
S. Posterior	T. Hemoglobin	U. Anterior
V. Implant	W. Epithelium	X. Eosinophil
Y. Hemoconcentration	Z. Antecubital fossa	

Provide the word that best matches each clue.

27. HIV _____ Human Immunodeficiency Virus

28. LANCET _____ A small pointed blade usually with two edges used for incising or puncturing.

29. THERAPEUTIC _____ Pertaining to results obtained through treatment; having medicinal or healing properties; a healing agent.

30. AEROSOL CANISTERS   Enclosed containers used to hold specimen tubes for centrifugation.

31. BLOOD COUNT   The determination of the proper number of red blood cells, white blood cells and platelets are present in the patient's blood.

32. VACUTAINER HOLDER   A cylindrical shaped holder that accepts a Vacutainer tube on one end and a Vacutainer needle on the other.

33. ANAEROBIC   Growing, living or occurring in the absence of molecular oxygen; pertaining to an anaerobe.

34. PRONE   Lying face down; opposed to supine.

35. FASTING   Without eating. Some laboratory tests are performed on "fasting" blood specimens such as sugar (glucose) levels and tolerance tests such as glucose, lactose and dextrose.

36. MICROCAPILLARY   Referring to collection of blood specimens by puncturing capillaries, usually in the heel of infants or the fingers of children and adults.

37. PERITONEAL DIALYSIS   Dialysis through the peritoneum.

38. CARBAMATE HEMOGLOBIN   The hemoglobin compound bound with carbon dioxide in the red blood cells.

39. ASEPTIC   The absence of microorganisms. By contrast, something that just discourages the growth of microorganisms is antiseptic.

40. SCLEROSIS   A hardening, especially from inflammation and certain disease states. Though sclerosis may occur in many areas of the body, the term is most often associated with blood vessels.

41. ETIOLOGY   The cause or origin of a disease or disorder.

42. ANTIPLATELET AGENT   Medications that, like aspirin, reduce the tendency of platelets in the blood to clump and clot.

43. PHLEBITIS   Inflammation of a vein. The condition is marked by infiltration of the layers of the vein and the formation of a clot. It produces edema, stiffness and pain in the affected area.

44. HEMATOCRIT   The ratio of the total red blood cell volume to the total blood volume and expressed as a percentage.

45. HUMORAL   Pertaining to elements dissolved in blood or body fluids, e.g., homoral immunity from antibodies in the blood as opposed to cellular immunity.

46. CENTRIFUGE   A laboratory apparatus that separates mixed samples into homogenous component layers by spinning them at high speed.

47. RED BLOOD CELL   The component of the blood that contains hemoglobin which is responsible for oxygen and carbon dioxide exchange.

48. SYNCOPE   Fainting; a temporary loss of consciousness due to a reduction of blood to the brain.

49. STAT   Abbreviation for the Latin word statim, meaning immediately.

50. CLOT   A semisolid mass of blood found inside or outside the body.

51. PIPET   A glass or transparent plastic tube used to accurately measure small amounts of liquid.

52. PARAFILM   A thin film of paraffin used primarily in the laboratory to seal open containers such as test tubes.

A. Aseptic	B. Sclerosis	C. Carbamate hemoglobin
D. Antiplatelet agent	E. Microcapillary	F. Centrifuge
G. Blood count	H. Aerosol canisters	I. HIV
J. Therapeutic	K. Lancet	L. Peritoneal dialysis
M. Parafilm	N. Red blood cell	O. Anaerobic
P. Etiology	Q. Hematocrit	R. Stat
S. Pipet	T. Fasting	U. Prone
V. Phlebitis	W. Vacutainer Holder	X. Clot
Y. Syncope	Z. Humoral	

Provide the word that best matches each clue.

53. PHAGOCYTOSIS   A process where polymorphonuclear leukocytes, monocytes, and macrophages combine with lysosomes within the cell cytoplasm to digest and destroy a particulate.

54. HUMORAL   Pertaining to elements dissolved in blood or body fluids, e.g., homoral immunity from antibodies in the blood as opposed to cellular immunity.

55. LEUKOCYTE   White blood cells.

56. TOURNIQUET — A constrictive band, placed over an extremity to distend veins for blood aspiration or intravenous injections.

57. PLATELET — Also known as a thrombocyte, this is a particulate component of the blood known for its involvement in blood coagulation.

58. APHERESIS — A technique in which blood products are separated from a donor and the desired elements collected and the rest returned to the donor.

59. ASPIRATE — As it relates to blood drawing, the material that is withdrawn with a negative pressure apparatus (syringe).

60. BLOOD CULTURE — A test which involves the incubation of a blood specimen overnight to determine if bacteria are present.

61. VEIN — Blood vessels carrying blood to the heart. Blood contained within these vessels is generally bound with carbon dioxide which will be exchanged for oxygen in the lungs.

62. CIRCULATION — The movement of fluid in a regular or circuitous course.

63. LYTES — A substance that will acquire the capacity to conduct electricity when put into solution. Electrolytes include sodium, potassium, chloride, calcium and phosphate.

64. WHOLE BLOOD — Blood from which none of the elements have been removed.

65. PARAFILM — A thin film of paraffin used primarily in the laboratory to seal open containers such as test tubes.

66. ARTERY — Blood vessel carrying blood away from the heart. Arterial blood is normally full of oxygen.

67. CARBAMATE HEMOGLOBIN — The hemoglobin compound bound with carbon dioxide in the red blood cells.

68. HYPOGLYCEMIA — An abnormally low glucose level in the blood.

69. MEAN CORPUSCULAR VOLUME — Average volume of red blood cells.

70. ABSORB — To suck up, as through pores.

71. GLUCOSE _____ The sugar measured in blood and urine specimens to determine the presence or absence of diabetes. Glucose is the product of carbohydrate metabolism and is the chief source of energy for all living organisms.

72. ELECTROLYTE _____ A substance that will acquire the capacity to conduct electricity when put into solution.

73. CYTOPLASM _____ The liquid portion of a cell including organelles and inclusions suspended in it. It is the site of most chemical activities of the cell.

74. SYNCOPE _____ Fainting; a temporary loss of consciousness due to a reduction of blood to the brain.

75. VACUOLE _____ Any small space of cavity formed in the protoplasm of a cell.

76. COAGULATE _____ The process of clot formation. Part of an important host defense mechanism call hemostasis.

77. MONOCYTE _____ A mononuclear, phagocytic leukocyte.

78. ANTERIOR _____ Toward the front or in front of.

A. Tourniquet
B. Cytoplasm
C. Parafilm
D. Anterior
E. Vein
F. Platelet
G. Humoral
H. Circulation
I. Electrolyte
J. Vacuole
K. Lytes
L. Absorb
M. Aspirate
N. Mean Corpuscular Volume
O. Glucose
P. Coagulate
Q. Carbamate hemoglobin
R. Monocyte
S. Hypoglycemia
T. Leukocyte
U. Syncope
V. Phagocytosis
W. Blood culture
X. Whole blood
Y. Apheresis
Z. Artery

Provide the word that best matches each clue.

79. CITRATE PHOSPHATE DEXTROSE _____ An anticoagulant.

80. FIBRINOGEN _____ The protein from which fibrin is formed.

81. HEMOSTASIS _____ The cessation of bleeding, either by vasoconstriction and coagulation or by surgical means.

82. ANTIPLATELET AGENT _____ Medications that, like aspirin, reduce the tendency of platelets in the blood to clump and clot.

83. HEMOLYSIS _____ The breaking of the red blood cells membrane releasing free hemoglobin into the circulating blood.

84.	WHITE BLOOD CELL COUNT	The number of white blood cells (leukocytes) found in the peripheral blood and measured per cubic millimeter.
85.	ANTIHEMOPHILIC FACTOR	A type of coagulation (clotting) factors.
86.	VENULE	A very tiny vein, continuous with the capillaries. Compare with arteriole.
87.	BLOOD CULTURE	A test which involves the incubation of a blood specimen overnight to determine if bacteria are present.
88.	SYNCOPE	Fainting; a temporary loss of consciousness due to a reduction of blood to the brain.
89.	INVITRO	Outside the living body; inside a glass; observable in a test tube.
90.	ARTERY	Blood vessel carrying blood away from the heart. Arterial blood is normally full of oxygen.
91.	CIRCULATORY SYSTEM	The circulatory system is composed of the heart, arteries, capillaries and veins.
92.	CIRCULATION	The movement of fluid in a regular or circuitous course.
93.	DORSAL	Denoting a position more toward the back surface than some other object of reference; same as posterior in human anatomy.
94.	CITRIC ACID CYCLE	A group or series of enzymatic reactions in living aerobic organisms that results in the production of energy.
95.	BLOOD CLOT	The conversion of blood from a liquid form to solid through the process of coagulation.
96.	IMPLANT	An object or material, such as tissue, partially or totally inserted or grafted into the body of a recipient.
97.	BACTEREMIA	The presence of viable bacteria circulating in the bloodstream. Diagnosed with blood cultures.
98.	COLLATERAL CIRCULATION	Blood which infuses an area through a secondary or accessory route.
99.	VENTRAL	Pertaining to the front side of the body.

100. EPITHELIUM _____ The outside layer of cells that covers all the free, open surfaces of the body including the skin, and mucous membranes that communicate with the outside of the body.

101. ANAPHYLAXIS _____ An acute, generalized life-threatening allergic or hypersensitive reaction.

102. HEPATITIS _____ Inflammation of the liver.

103. PROXIMAL _____ Nearest to any other point of reference.

104. FISTULA _____ An abnormal passageway usually between two internal organs. Such passages may be created experimentally for obtaining body secretions for study.

A. Syncope	B. Citrate phosphate dextrose	C. Anaphylaxis
D. Epithelium	E. White blood cell count	F. Fistula
G. Ventral	H. Antihemophilic factor	I. Hemostasis
J. Circulatory System	K. Artery	L. Bacteremia
M. Citric Acid Cycle	N. Blood clot	O. Invitro
P. Implant	Q. Collateral circulation	R. Proximal
S. Antiplatelet agent	T. Venule	U. Circulation
V. Dorsal	W. Hepatitis	X. Hemolysis
Y. Fibrinogen	Z. Blood culture	

Provide the word that best matches each clue.

105. PROPHYLAXIS _____ A preventative treatment.

106. BLEEDING TIME _____ A test which measures the time it takes for small blood vessels to close off and bleeding to stop.

107. VEIN _____ Blood vessels carrying blood to the heart. Blood contained within these vessels is generally bound with carbon dioxide which will be exchanged for oxygen in the lungs.

108. INVIVO _____ Inside the living body.

109. MACROPHAGE _____ Any of the many forms of mononuclear phagocytes found in tissues and originating from stem cells in the bone marrow. In normal circulation, the monocyte may be categorized as a macrophage.

110. SCLEROSIS _____ A hardening, especially from inflammation and certain disease states. Though sclerosis may occur in many areas of the body, the term is most often associated with blood vessels.

111. HEPATITIS A — Usually a self-limited viral disease. Transmission is usually the result of poor hygiene and most often through the fecal-oral route.

112. MEDIAL — Pertaining to the middle aspect; closer to the midline of the body or structure.

113. HEPATITIS C — The most common form of hepatitis after blood transfusion. It is also the most prevalent form resulting from needle sharing by drug abusers.

114. ARTERIOVENOUS FISTULA — The surgical joining of an artery and a vein under the skin for hemodialysis.

115. FLASH BACK — Relative to venipunctures, the appearance of a small amount of blood in the neck of a syringe or the tubing of a butterfly. This is a sign that the vein has been properly accessed.

116. BRUISE — A bruise or ""contusion" is a traumatic injury of the soft tissues which results in breakage of the local capillaries and leakage of red blood cells.

117. PARAFILM — A thin film of paraffin used primarily in the laboratory to seal open containers such as test tubes.

118. BLOOD — The fluid in the body that contains red cells and white cells as well as platelets, proteins, plasma and other elements. It is transported throughout the body by the Circulatory System.

119. HYPODERMIC NEEDLE — A needle that attaches to a syringe for injections or withdrawal of fluids such as blood.

120. EDTA — A calcium chelating (binding) agent that is used as an anticoagulant for laboratory blood specimens. Also used in treatment of lead poisoning.

121. LYMPH — Fluid found in lymphatic vessels and nodes derived from tissue fluids. Lymph is collected from all parts of the body and returned to the blood by the lymphatic system.

122. THROMBOCYTOPENIA — Decrease in the number of blood platelets below normal values.

123. CENTRIFUGE — A laboratory apparatus that separates mixed samples into homogenous component layers by spinning them at high speed.

124. PHAGOCYTOSIS _____ A process where polymorphonuclear leukocytes, monocytes, and macrophages combine with lysosomes within the cell cytoplasm to digest and destroy a particulate.

125. CARBAMATE HEMOGLOBIN _____ The hemoglobin compound bound with carbon dioxide in the red blood cells.

126. HEPATITIS _____ Inflammation of the liver.

127. GRAFT _____ An implant or transplant of any tissue or organ.

128. BLOOD CLOTTING FACTOR _____ Any different protein factors which, when acting together, can form a blood clot shortly after platelets have broken at the site of the wound.

129. HUMORAL _____ Pertaining to elements dissolved in blood or body fluids, e.g., homoral immunity from antibodies in the blood as opposed to cellular immunity.

130. DIAPHORETIC _____ Formation of profuse perspiration (sweat). A symptom of syncope or vasovagal response.

A. Thrombocytopenia
D. Medial
G. Blood clotting factor
J. Hypodermic needle
M. Sclerosis
P. Carbamate hemoglobin
S. Phagocytosis
V. Humoral
Y. Vein

B. Parafilm
E. Macrophage
H. Graft
K. Hepatitis
N. Hepatitis C
Q. Invivo
T. Bleeding time
W. Lymph
Z. Prophylaxis

C. EDTA
F. Blood
I. Diaphoretic
L. Flash back
O. Hepatitis A
R. Centrifuge
U. Bruise
X. Arteriovenous fistula

Provide the word that best matches each clue.

131. VACUOLE _____ Any small space of cavity formed in the protoplasm of a cell.

132. SCLEROSIS _____ A hardening, especially from inflammation and certain disease states. Though sclerosis may occur in many areas of the body, the term is most often associated with blood vessels.

133. EPIDEMIOLOGY _____ The science concerned with the study of factors influencing the distribution of disease and their causes in a defined population.

134. VACUTAINER _____ A trade name now a generic term used to describe equipment used to automatically aspirate blood from a vessel by venipuncture.

135. HYPERSENSITIVITY — A state in which the body reacts with an exaggerated immune response to a foreign substance. Reactions are classified as delayed or immediate types.

136. THROMBOCYTE — Also known as a platelet, this is a particulate component of the blood, approximately 2-4 microns in diameter and known for its involvement in blood coagulation.

137. CITRIC ACID CYCLE — A group or series of enzymatic reactions in living aerobic organisms that results in the production of energy.

138. ABSORB — To suck up, as through pores.

139. HYPOGLYCEMIA — An abnormally low glucose level in the blood.

140. CARBAMATE HEMOGLOBIN — The hemoglobin compound bound with carbon dioxide in the red blood cells.

141. VENTRAL — Pertaining to the front side of the body.

142. STANDARD PRECAUTIONS — Precautions that are designed for the care of all patients in hospitals regardless of their diagnosis or presumed infection status.

143. SYNCOPE — Fainting; a temporary loss of consciousness due to a reduction of blood to the brain.

144. ADSORB — To attract and retain other material on the surface.

145. BLOOD CLOT — The conversion of blood from a liquid form to solid through the process of coagulation.

146. VASCULAR GRAFT — A type of an arteriovenous fistula consisting of either a venous autograft or synthetic tube which is grafted to the artery and vein.

147. CEPHALIC VEIN — A large vein of the arm that empties into the axillary vein

148. PALPATE — To examine or feel by the hand. In relation to venipunctures, this technique is used to "feel" a vein which will tend to rebound when slight pressure is applied with the finger.

149. HEPATITIS B — An acute form of hepatitis caused by a virus. The virus is shed in body fluids of chronic and acute patients as well as asymptomatic carriers.

150. INVIVO — Inside the living body.

151. ERYTHROCYTE — Cells that carry oxygen to all parts of the body.

152. TOURNIQUET — A constrictive band, placed over an extremity to distend veins for blood aspiration or intravenous injections.

153. COAGULATE — The process of clot formation. Part of an important host defense mechanism call hemostasis.

154. FIBRINOGEN — The protein from which fibrin is formed.

155. ALBUMIN — Main protein in human blood.

156. MACROPHAGE — Any of the many forms of mononuclear phagocytes found in tissues and originating from stem cells in the bone marrow. In normal circulation, the monocyte may be categorized as a macrophage.

A. Blood clot	B. Hypersensitivity	C. Fibrinogen
D. Hypoglycemia	E. Vacuole	F. Palpate
G. Standard Precautions	H. Erythrocyte	I. Macrophage
J. Vascular graft	K. Carbamate hemoglobin	L. Thrombocyte
M. Cephalic vein	N. Albumin	O. Vacutainer
P. Absorb	Q. Syncope	R. Coagulate
S. Ventral	T. Sclerosis	U. Adsorb
V. Hepatitis B	W. Invivo	X. Tourniquet
Y. Citric Acid Cycle	Z. Epidemiology	

Provide the word that best matches each clue.

157. SYNCOPE — Fainting; a temporary loss of consciousness due to a reduction of blood to the brain.

158. CANNULA — A tube for insertion into a duct or cavity.

159. COMPLETE BLOOD COUNT — The number of red blood cells, white blood cells and platelets (per cubic millimeter) that are present in the patient's sample of blood is determined.

160. AEROSOL CANISTERS — Enclosed containers used to hold specimen tubes for centrifugation.

161. HEPATITIS B — An acute form of hepatitis caused by a virus. The virus is shed in body fluids of chronic and acute patients as well as asymptomatic carriers.

162. PERITONEAL DIALYSIS — Dialysis through the peritoneum.

163. FIBRIN — The protein formed during normal blood clotting that is the essence of the clot.

164. ARTERY — Blood vessel carrying blood away from the heart. Arterial blood is normally full of oxygen.

165. PALLOR — Paleness; decrease of absence of skin color.

166. TRANSPLANT — An organ or tissue taken from the body for grafting into another part of the same body or into another individual.

167. CYTOPLASM _____ The liquid portion of a cell including organelles and inclusions suspended in it. It is the site of most chemical activities of the cell.

168. CARBAMATE HEMOGLOBIN _____ The hemoglobin compound bound with carbon dioxide in the red blood cells.

169. ANEMIA _____ The condition of having less than the normal number of red blood cells or hemoglobin in the blood.

170. BLOOD COUNT _____ The determination of the proper number of red blood cells, white blood cells and platelets are present in the patient's blood.

171. LYMPHEDEMA _____ A type of swelling which occurs in lymphatic tissue when excess fluid collects in the arms or legs because the lymph nodes or vessels are blocked or removed.

172. CONTAMINATION _____ The soiling by inferior material, as by the introduction of organisms into a wound.

173. CIRCULATORY SYSTEM _____ The circulatory system is composed of the heart, arteries, capillaries and veins.

174. DIFFERENTIAL _____ A count made on a stained blood smear of the proportion of the different leukocytes (WBC's) and expressed as a percentage.

175. ACUTE _____ Of short duration. Rapid and abbreviated in onset.

176. BLIND STICK _____ Performing a venipuncture with no apparently visible or palpable vein.

177. PHLEBOTOMIST _____ One who practices phlebotomy.

178. THERAPEUTIC _____ Pertaining to results obtained through treatment; having medicinal or healing properties; a healing agent.

179. ECCHYMOSIS _____ The skin discoloration caused by a bruise (contusion).

180. ASPIRATE _____ As it relates to blood drawing, the material that is withdrawn with a negative pressure apparatus (syringe).

181. SCLEROSIS _____ A hardening, especially from inflammation and certain disease states. Though sclerosis may occur in many areas of the body, the term is most often associated with blood vessels.

182. ADSORB _____ To attract and retain other material on the surface.

A. Ecchymosis   B. Syncope   C. Blind stick
D. Therapeutic   E. Adsorb   F. Carbamate hemoglobin

G. Cannula
J. Cytoplasm
M. Complete blood count
P. Artery
S. Phlebotomist
V. Blood count
Y. Transplant

H. Pallor
K. Lymphedema
N. Aspirate
Q. Peritoneal dialysis
T. Aerosol canisters
W. Differential
Z. Acute

I. Anemia
L. Circulatory System
O. Sclerosis
R. Contamination
U. Fibrin
X. Hepatitis B

Provide the word that best matches each clue.

183. LEUKOCYTE — White blood cells.

184. HEMATOCRIT — The ratio of the total red blood cell volume to the total blood volume and expressed as a percentage.

185. HYPODERMIC NEEDLE — A needle that attaches to a syringe for injections or withdrawal of fluids such as blood.

186. NOSOCOMIAL INFECTION — A hospital-borne infection. An infection whose origin is from within the hospital environment.

187. MONOCYTE — A mononuclear, phagocytic leukocyte.

188. CENTRIFUGE — A laboratory apparatus that separates mixed samples into homogenous component layers by spinning them at high speed.

189. VEIN — Blood vessels carrying blood to the heart. Blood contained within these vessels is generally bound with carbon dioxide which will be exchanged for oxygen in the lungs.

190. BLOOD COUNT — The determination of the proper number of red blood cells, white blood cells and platelets are present in the patient's blood.

191. PATHOGENIC — Having the capability of producing disease.

192. CONTACT PRECAUTIONS — This precaution is for specified patients known or suspected to be infected or colonized with microorganisms that can be transmitted by direct contact with the patient.

193. HEPATITIS — Inflammation of the liver.

194. DISTAL — Remote, farther from any point of reference, opposed to proximal

195. VASOCONSTRICTION — A decrease in the inside diameter of especially arterioles leading to a decrease in blood flow to a part.

196. VASCULAR — Pertaining to or composed of blood vessels. The vascular system is composed of the heart, blood vessels, lymphatics and their parts considered collectively.

197. VENTRAL _____ Pertaining to the front side of the body.

198. PALPATE _____ To examine or feel by the hand. In relation to venipunctures, this technique is used to "feel" a vein which will tend to rebound when slight pressure is applied with the finger.

199. THROMBUS _____ A blood clot obstructing a blood vessel or a cavity of the heart. Heparin and Warfarin Sodium are being used to assist in dissolving or preventing clot formations.

200. ALLERGEN _____ An antigenic substance capable of producing an immediate-type hypersensitivity (allergy).

201. PHLEBITIS _____ Inflammation of a vein. The condition is marked by infiltration of the layers of the vein and the formation of a clot. It produces edema, stiffness and pain in the affected area.

202. VENIPUNCTURE _____ The puncture of a vein for any purpose

203. BLEEDING TIME _____ A test which measures the time it takes for small blood vessels to close off and bleeding to stop.

204. SUPINE _____ Lying down with the face up; opposed to prone.

205. APHERESIS _____ A technique in which blood products are separated from a donor and the desired elements collected and the rest returned to the donor.

206. HEMATOMA _____ A localized collection of blood within tissue due to leakage from the wall of a blood vessel, producing a bluish discoloration (ecchymosis)and pain.

207. ALBUMIN _____ Main protein in human blood.

208. FAINT _____ A sudden loss of consciousness.

A. Vasoconstriction	B. Pathogenic	C. Centrifuge
D. Supine	E. Contact Precautions	F. Palpate
G. Nosocomial infection	H. Faint	I. Hepatitis
J. Vein	K. Apheresis	L. Distal
M. Bleeding time	N. Thrombus	O. Blood count
P. Hematoma	Q. Albumin	R. Venipuncture
S. Allergen	T. Phlebitis	U. Monocyte
V. Ventral	W. Hypodermic needle	X. Hematocrit
Y. Leukocyte	Z. Vascular	

Provide the word that best matches each clue.

209. REVERSE ISOLATION — An isolation procedure designed to protect the patient from contracting disease. Frequently used for transplant patients or for patients whose immune response has been greatly reduced.

210. BLOOD FILM — A sample of blood is applied to a microscope slide and then studied under the microscope.

211. STANDARD PRECAUTIONS — Precautions that are designed for the care of all patients in hospitals regardless of their diagnosis or presumed infection status.

212. WARFARIN SODIUM — The sodium salt of warfarin, one of the synthetic anticoagulants. Coumadin is a brand name.

213. SCLEROSIS — A hardening, especially from inflammation and certain disease states. Though sclerosis may occur in many areas of the body, the term is most often associated with blood vessels.

214. VASOCONSTRICTION — A decrease in the inside diameter of especially arterioles leading to a decrease in blood flow to a part.

215. HEPATITIS — Inflammation of the liver.

216. ADSORB — To attract and retain other material on the surface.

217. CLOT — A semisolid mass of blood found inside or outside the body.

218. EDEMA — The swelling of soft tissues caused by excess fluid accumulation.

219. BLOOD TRANSFER DEVICE — A safety device designed to transfer blood from one container into another.

220. VASOVAGAL RESPONSE — A transient vascular and neurogenic reaction marked by pallor, nausea, sweating, slowing heart rate and a rapid fall in arterial blood pressure which may result in loss of consciousness.

221. COUMADIN — A brand name for warfarin sodium.

222. ASEPTIC — The absence of microorganisms. By contrast, something that just discourages the growth of microorganisms is antiseptic.

223. PALLOR — Paleness; decrease of absence of skin color.

224. PLATELETPHERESIS _____ The selective separation and removal of platelets from withdrawn blood. The remainder of the blood is re-transfused back into the donor.

225. RED BLOOD CELL _____ The component of the blood that contains hemoglobin which is responsible for oxygen and carbon dioxide exchange.

226. LEUKOCYTE _____ Called White Blood Cells. A variety of cells within the blood and bone marrow whose general purpose is to help in fighting infection.

227. FLEXION _____ The process of bending or the state of being bent. Flexion of the fingers results in a clenched fist.

228. ANTERIOR _____ Toward the front or in front of.

229. CHELATE _____ Combining with a metallic ion into a ring complex.

230. ANAPHYLAXIS _____ An acute, generalized life-threatening allergic or hypersensitive reaction.

231. CEPHALIC VEIN _____ A large vein of the arm that empties into the axillary vein

232. CONTACT PRECAUTIONS _____ This precaution is for specified patients known or suspected to be infected or colonized with microorganisms that can be transmitted by direct contact with the patient.

233. LATERAL _____ A position farther from the midline of the body or another reference structure.

234. MEDIAL CUBITAL VEIN _____ The forearm vein most commonly used for venipuncture because it is generally the largest and best-anchored vein

A. Anterior
E. Standard Precautions
I. Vasovagal response
M. Coumadin
Q. Edema
U. Clot
Y. Contact Precautions

B. Leukocyte
F. Reverse isolation
J. Plateletpheresis
N. Chelate
R. Hepatitis
V. Red blood cell
Z. Warfarin sodium

C. Aseptic
G. Pallor
K. Flexion
O. Adsorb
S. Blood transfer device
W. Lateral

D. Anaphylaxis
H. Blood film
L. Medial cubital vein
P. Sclerosis
T. Cephalic vein
X. Vasoconstriction

Word Search

1. *Find the hidden words. The words have been placed horizontally, vertically, or diagonally. When you locate a word, draw a circle around it.*

A	A	N	A	E	R	O	B	I	C	K	A	S	P	I	R	A	T	E	Q
L	I	Z	W	A	R	F	A	R	I	N	S	O	D	I	U	M	D	P	T
Y	L	J	W	N	T	S	Q	I	E	X	K	S	M	V	D	V	M	A	N
T	I	F	I	S	T	U	L	A	Q	B	A	S	A	L	S	T	A	T	E
E	C	A	R	B	O	X	Y	H	E	M	O	G	L	O	B	I	N	H	B
S	L	A	M	I	N	A	R	F	L	O	W	H	O	O	D	O	C	O	H
E	R	Y	T	H	R	O	C	Y	T	E	H	U	M	O	R	A	L	G	X
E	Z	O	P	O	S	T	E	R	I	O	R	S	P	E	L	F	Y	E	N
K	D	S	A	D	V	A	S	C	U	L	A	R	G	R	A	F	T	N	P
F	A	S	T	I	N	G	U	T	O	U	R	N	I	Q	U	E	T	I	O
E	N	L	V	T	H	E	R	A	P	E	U	T	I	C	Z	W	P	C	D
U	R	M	V	A	C	U	T	A	I	N	E	R	H	O	L	D	E	R	S

1. An abnormal passageway usually between two internal organs. Such passages may be created experimentally for obtaining body secretions for study.
2. A type of an arteriovenous fistula consisting of either a venous autograft or synthetic tube which is grafted to the artery and vein.
3. Growing, living or occurring in the absence of molecular oxygen; pertaining to an anaerobe.
4. Situated at the back (dorsal) part of a structure.
5. The sodium salt of warfarin, one of the synthetic anticoagulants. Coumadin is a brand name.
6. Having the capability of producing disease.
7. The state of the body early in the morning, approximately 12 hours after the last ingestion of food or other nutrition.
8. Pertaining to elements dissolved in blood or body fluids, e.g., homoral immunity from antibodies in the blood as opposed to cellular immunity.
9. Hemoglobin which has been bound with carbon monoxide, which has an affinity for hemoglobin 200 times greater than oxygen.
10. Pertaining to results obtained through treatment; having medicinal or healing properties; a healing agent.
11. A constrictive band, placed over an extremity to distend veins for blood aspiration or intravenous injections.
12. A cylindrical shaped holder that accepts a Vacutainer tube on one end and a Vacutainer needle on the other.
13. Cells that carry oxygen to all parts of the body.
14. A substance that will acquire the capacity to conduct electricity when put into solution. Electrolytes include sodium, potassium, chloride, calcium and phosphate.
15. As it relates to blood drawing, the material that is withdrawn with a negative pressure apparatus (syringe).
16. Safety cabinets with air flow in such a direction as to carry any harmful materials or fumes away from the worker.
17. Without eating. Some laboratory tests are performed on "fasting" blood specimens such as sugar (glucose) levels and tolerance tests such as glucose, lactose and dextrose.

A. Aspirate
E. Therapeutic
I. Vascular graft
M. Basal state
Q. Anaerobic

B. Carboxyhemoglobin
F. Tourniquet
J. Fistula
N. Humoral

C. Lytes
G. Pathogenic
K. Vacutainer Holder
O. Erythrocyte

D. Laminar flow hood
H. Posterior
L. Fasting
P. Warfarin sodium

2. *Find the hidden words. The words have been placed horizontally, vertically, or diagonally. When you locate a word, draw a circle around it.*

W	H	P	P	O	T	B	P	P	T	A	Z	M	N	H	I	S	R	U	L
N	V	A	C	U	T	A	I	N	E	R	T	U	B	E		F	B	G	Y
L	A	B	L	S	X	U	M	J	P	T	V	A	R	M	D	C	L	J	M
Y	T	L	Y	Y	T	G	Q	D	A	E	A	N	C	O	L	I	J	N	P
M	E	O	T	R	Y	K	O	Y	L	R	S	H	F	D	Q	T	D	X	H
P	J	O	E	I	H	M	L	L	M	I	C	W	A	I	V	R	J	U	O
H	C	D	S	N	F	T	J	M	A	O	U	D	I	A	A	A	K	F	C
E	T	C	H	G	S	P	D	S	R	L	L	B	N	L	C	T	V	N	Y
D	B	E	B	E	N	G	N	B	J	E	A	N	T	Y	U	E	F	C	T
E	B	L	G	H	V	T	T	S	Z	G	R	Q	D	S	O	S	U	Z	E
M	I	L	F	A	Y	G	L	U	C	O	S	E		I	L	O	T	Q	G
A	R	Y	A	P	H	E	R	E	S	I	S	J	U	S	E	V	O	O	E

1. The removal of certain components of the blood by diffusion through a semipermeable membrane.
2. Blood sample tubes containing a vacuum. When the tube stopper is pierced by a Vacutainer needle which has been properly positioned in a vein, the vacuum draws blood into the tube.
3. The sugar measured in blood and urine specimens to determine the presence or absence of diabetes. Glucose is the product of carbohydrate metabolism and is the chief source of energy for all living organisms.
4. A type of swelling which occurs in lymphatic tissue when excess fluid collects in the arms or legs because the lymph nodes or vessels are blocked or removed.
5. There are three main types of cell in the blood stream. The red cell, which carries oxygen, the white cell, which fights infections and the platelet, which helps prevent bleeding.
6. Any small space of cavity formed in the protoplasm of a cell.
7. A small branch of an artery that leads to a capillary. Also, see capillary.
8. Referring to the palm surface or side of the hand
9. A substance that will acquire the capacity to conduct electricity when put into solution. Electrolytes include sodium, potassium, chloride, calcium and phosphate.
10. Hemoglobin which has been bound with carbon monoxide, which has an affinity for hemoglobin 200 times greater than oxygen.
11. A sudden loss of consciousness.
12. Pertaining to or composed of blood vessels. The vascular system is composed of the heart, blood vessels, lymphatics and their parts considered collectively.
13. A technique in which blood products are separated from a donor and the desired elements collected and the rest returned to the donor.
14. A cylindrical shaped holder that accepts a Vacutainer tube on one end and a Vacutainer needle on the other.
15. An instrument used to inject fluids into or aspirate fluids from any vessel or cavity.
16. The number of red blood cells, white blood cells and platelets (per cubic millimeter) that are present in the patient's sample of blood is determined.
17. A compound that is an intermediate in the citric acid cycle (Krebs cycle or glycolysis). Citrate chelates (binds) calcium ions, preventing blood clotting and, thus, is an effective anticoagulant.
18. Any of the mononuclear, nonphagocytic leukocytes, found in the blood and lymph, which are the body's immunologically competent cells.

A. Vacuole
E. Lymphocyte
I. Complete blood count
M. Arteriole
Q. Lytes
B. Glucose
F. Apheresis
J. Carboxyhemoglobin
N. Lymphedema
R. Vacutainer Holder
C. Faint
G. Hemodialysis
K. Vascular
O. Palmar
D. Citrate
H. Syringe
L. Blood cell
P. Vacutainer tube

3. *Find the hidden words. The words have been placed horizontally, vertically, or diagonally. When you locate a word, draw a circle around it.*

J	W	G	B	L	O	O	D	B	P	P	R	O	N	E	I	Y	S	L	M
Y	V	K	S	U	E	J	J	G	O	N	X	I	A	L	Z	M	T	L	U
P	J	L	Y	X	E	K	P	C	S	G	H	L	T	R	J	T	A	N	A
S	I	Y	M	M	O	A	L	O	T	E	F	F	L	U	E	N	T		I
Q	C	A	R	B	A	M	A	T	E	H	E	M	O	G	L	O	B	I	N
G	D	Y	W	U	P	N	T	I	R	G	L	U	C	O	S	E		C	B
Z	X	G	I	R	Y	B	E	X	I	N	C	O	N	T	U	S	I	O	N
W	S	U	P	I	N	E	L	N	O	O	M	K	G	D	N	I	D	U	K
K	P	N	E	Z	I	L	E	R	R	D	A	N	A	E	R	O	B	I	C
D	B	R	M	A	V	C	T	P	U	E	C	C	H	Y	M	O	S	I	S
O	N	D	A	L	C	R	Q	A	N	A	P	H	Y	L	A	X	I	S	N
P	O	V	I	D	O	N	E	I	O	D	I	N	E	Q	Q	C	F	F	H

1. The hemoglobin compound bound with carbon dioxide in the red blood cells.
2. The sugar measured in blood and urine specimens to determine the presence or absence of diabetes. Glucose is the product of carbohydrate metabolism and is the chief source of energy for all living organisms.
3. An outflow, usually of fluid.
4. Lying down with the face up; opposed to prone.
5. Situated at the back (dorsal) part of a structure.
6. Also known as a thrombocyte, this is a particulate component of the blood known for its involvement in blood coagulation.
7. The fluid in the body that contains red cells and white cells as well as platelets, proteins, plasma and other elements. It is transported throughout the body by the Circulatory System.
8. An acute, generalized life-threatening allergic or hypersensitive reaction.
9. Used as a topical antiseptic, this is a compound made by reacting iodine with povidone which slowly releases iodine.
10. Dialysis through the peritoneum.
11. Abbreviation for the Latin word statim, meaning immediately.
12. A decrease in the fluid content of the blood (plasma), resulting in an increase in concentration. This is determined by an increase in the hematocrit. Caused by a filtration of plasma into body tissues and often created by dehydration.
13. Growing, living or occurring in the absence of molecular oxygen; pertaining to an anaerobe.
14. A decrease in the inside diameter of especially arterioles leading to a decrease in blood flow to a part.
15. A bruise or injury without a break in the skin.
16. A hospital-borne infection. An infection whose origin is from within the hospital environment.
17. Lying face down; opposed to supine.
18. The skin discoloration caused by a bruise (contusion).
19. A type of coagulation (clotting) factors.

A. Effluent
E. Vasoconstriction
I. Contusion
M. Prone
Q. Anaphylaxis

B. Glucose
F. Peritoneal dialysis
J. Stat
N. Anaerobic
R. Platelet

C. Blood
G. Posterior
K. Antihemophilic factor
O. Ecchymosis
S. Povidone iodine

D. Hemoconcentration
H. Carbamate hemoglobin
L. Supine
P. Nosocomial infection

4. *Find the hidden words. The words have been placed horizontally, vertically, or diagonally. When you locate a word, draw a circle around it.*

Q	O	I	S	E	A	N	A	P	H	Y	L	A	X	I	S	S	P	B	C
Q	H	A	R	V	E	S	T	I	N	G	F	J	T	M	X	A	J	L	O
L	B	X	H	E	P	A	T	I	T	I	S	C	O	P	H	H	K	O	H
E	P	L	A	S	M	A	E	L	M	A	S	E	P	T	I	C	J	O	O
P	V	V	B	B	X	W	P	H	L	E	B	I	T	I	S	K	W	D	R
I	M	M	J	P	O	V	I	D	O	N	E	I	O	D	I	N	E	V	T
D	H	Y	P	O	D	E	R	M	I	C	N	E	E	D	L	E	L	E	I
E	C	O	N	T	A	C	T	P	R	E	C	A	U	T	I	O	N	S	N
R	V	E	N	E	S	E	C	T	I	O	N	B	Y	W	Y	Q	R	S	G
M	P	A	L	P	A	T	E	P	U	Q	V	E	N	O	U	S	D	E	E
I	O	E	Q	P	Z	J	E	E	F	F	L	U	E	N	T		D	L	H
S	S	T	A	N	D	A	R	D	P	R	E	C	A	U	T	I	O	N	S

1. Opening of a vein for collecting blood.
2. All the vessels lined with endothelium through which blood circulates.
3. Used as a topical antiseptic, this is a compound made by reacting iodine with povidone which slowly releases iodine.
4. In epidemiology, a group of individuals who share common characteristics.
5. The collection and preservation of tissues or cells from a donor for transplantation.
6. The most common form of hepatitis after blood transfusion. It is also the most prevalent form resulting from needle sharing by drug abusers.
7. The upper or outer layer of the two main layers of cells that make up the skin.
8. Precautions that are designed for the care of all patients in hospitals regardless of their diagnosis or presumed infection status.
9. Pertaining to the veins, or blood passing through them.
10. A set of procedures and protocols designed to protect the healthcare worker which uses the basic concept that each patient must be treated as though they were infected with an infectious disease.

11. This precaution is for specified patients known or suspected to be infected or colonized with microorganisms that can be transmitted by direct contact with the patient.
12. An outflow, usually of fluid.
13. Inflammation of a vein. The condition is marked by infiltration of the layers of the vein and the formation of a clot. It produces edema, stiffness and pain in the affected area.
14. The absence of microorganisms. By contrast, something that just discourages the growth of microorganisms is antiseptic.
15. The fluid portion of the blood in which the cellular components are suspended. Plasma contains coagulation factors used in the clotting of blood as opposed to serum.
16. An acute, generalized life-threatening allergic or hypersensitive reaction.
17. To examine or feel by the hand. In relation to venipunctures, this technique is used to "feel" a vein which will tend to rebound when slight pressure is applied with the finger.
18. A needle that attaches to a syringe for injections or withdrawal of fluids such as blood.

A. Cohorting
E. Blood vessel
I. Anaphylaxis
M. Epidermis
Q. Effluent

B. Palpate
F. Venous
J. Venesection
N. Povidone iodine
R. Contact Precautions

C. Hypodermic needle
G. Plasma
K. Universal Precautions
O. Harvesting

D. Hepatitis C
H. Aseptic
L. Standard Precautions
P. Phlebitis

5. *Find the hidden words. The words have been placed horizontally, vertically, or diagonally. When you locate a word, draw a circle around it.*

T	S	J	U	V	V	E	N	O	U	S	D	I	V	Q	M	D	X	Y	S
H	M	C	Y	T	O	P	L	A	S	M	C	H	R	O	M	A	T	I	N
E	N	Q	E	R	Y	T	H	R	O	C	Y	T	E	L	I	T	D	M	M
R	F	I	B	R	I	N	V	P	H	L	E	B	I	T	I	S	I	O	R
A	T	B	L	O	O	D	G	R	O	U	P	R	Q	N	X	A	A	N	H
P	G	V	E	N	U	L	E	A	S	E	P	T	I	C	K	E	L	O	M
E	I	J	B	T	S	E	B	U	I	V	Y	H	M	G	G	R	Y	C	W
U	S	D	Y	O	A	H	E	P	A	T	I	T	I	S	C	O	S	Y	K
T	Q	M	A	E	C	C	H	Y	M	O	S	I	S	Q	C	B	I	T	E
I	D	I	S	T	A	L	Q	K	O	B	R	O	P	Q	I	S	E	S
C	U	M	J	O	K	S	Y	N	C	O	P	E	Q	W	J	C	G	L	K
Q	F	E	H	W	L	Y	S	P	T	H	E	P	A	T	I	T	I	S	A

1. A very tiny vein, continuous with the capillaries. Compare with arteriole.
2. The process of cleansing the blood by passing it through a special machine. Dialysis is necessary when the kidneys are not able to filter the blood.
3. The liquid portion of a cell including organelles and inclusions suspended in it. It is the site of most chemical activities of the cell.
4. The skin discoloration caused by a bruise (contusion).
5. Remote, farther from any point of reference, opposed to proximal
6. Pertaining to results obtained through treatment; having medicinal or healing properties; a healing agent.
7. Usually a self-limited viral disease. Transmission is usually the result of poor hygiene and most often through the fecal-oral route.
8. Fainting; a temporary loss of consciousness due to a reduction of blood to the brain.
9. The protein formed during normal blood clotting that is the essence of the clot.
10. Pertaining to the veins, or blood passing through them.
11. A mononuclear, phagocytic leukocyte.
12. Inflammation of a vein. The condition is marked by infiltration of the layers of the vein and the formation of a clot. It produces edema, stiffness and pain in the affected area.
13. An inherited feature on the surface of the red blood cell. A series of related blood groups make up a blood group system such as the ABO system or the Rh system.
14. The most common form of hepatitis after blood transfusion. It is also the most prevalent form resulting from needle sharing by drug abusers.
15. Cells that carry oxygen to all parts of the body.
16. The more readily stainable portion of the cell nucleus. It is a DNA attached to a protein structure and is the carrier of genes in inheritance.
17. The absence of microorganisms. By contrast, something that just discourages the growth of microorganisms is antiseptic.
18. Having molecular oxygen present.

A. Therapeutic
B. Monocyte
C. Venule
D. Venous
E. Aerobic
F. Ecchymosis
G. Chromatin
H. Blood group
I. Fibrin
J. Aseptic
K. Syncope
L. Erythrocyte
M. Hepatitis A
N. Phlebitis
O. Hepatitis C
P. Dialysis
Q. Distal
R. Cytoplasm

6. *Find the hidden words. The words have been placed horizontally, vertically, or diagonally. When you locate a word, draw a circle around it.*

C	B	W	H	D	Y	H	O	F	E	P	I	T	H	E	L	I	U	M	C
H	C	C	E	L	V	C	O	N	T	A	M	I	N	A	T	I	O	N	O
I	E	A	M	E	R	Q	R	H	S	Y	S	T	E	M	F	Z	I	L	N
V	N	T	O	U	D	I	F	F	E	R	E	N	T	I	A	L	F	L	T
Z	T	H	S	K	A	S	P	I	R	A	T	E	A	P	Q	J	R	U	U
A	R	E	T	O	F	K	S	Y	R	I	N	G	E	P	I	P	E	T	S
C	I	T	A	C	F	F	Q	X	A	C	A	N	N	U	L	A	Z	S	I
L	F	E	S	Y	M	A	N	T	I	C	O	A	G	U	L	A	N	T	O
L	U	R	I	T	M	J	H	E	M	A	C	R	O	P	H	A	G	E	N
L	G	U	S	E	T	K	F	H	Y	P	O	G	L	Y	C	E	M	I	A
P	E	R	I	T	O	N	E	A	L	D	I	A	L	Y	S	I	S	V	W
C	O	M	P	L	E	T	E	B	L	O	O	D	C	O	U	N	T	R	Z

1. White blood cells.
2. An abnormally low glucose level in the blood.
3. Dialysis through the peritoneum.
4. A bruise or injury without a break in the skin.
5. The number of red blood cells, white blood cells and platelets (per cubic millimeter) that are present in the patient's sample of blood is determined.
6. An instrument used to inject fluids into or aspirate fluids from any vessel or cavity.
7. A thin, flexible tube. When a catheter is placed in a vein, it provides a pathway for giving drugs, nutrients, fluids, or blood products.
8. The soiling by inferior material, as by the introduction of organisms into a wound.
9. Human Immunodeficiency Virus
10. The most complex of all human blood groups and is responsible for serious hemolytic disease of the newborn.
11. A laboratory apparatus that separates mixed samples into homogenous component layers by spinning them at high speed.
12. A tube for insertion into a duct or cavity.
13. The outside layer of cells that covers all the free, open surfaces of the body including the skin, and mucous membranes that communicate with the outside of the body.
14. Any of the many forms of mononuclear phagocytes found in tissues and originating from stem cells in the bone marrow. In normal circulation, the monocyte may be categorized as a macrophage.
15. The cessation of bleeding, either by vasoconstriction and coagulation or by surgical means.
16. Any substance that prevents blood clotting.
17. A glass or transparent plastic tube used to accurately measure small amounts of liquid.
18. A count made on a stained blood smear of the proportion of the different leukocytes (WBC's) and expressed as a percentage.
19. As it relates to blood drawing, the material that is withdrawn with a negative pressure apparatus (syringe).

A. Anticoagulant
E. Rh System
I. Hypoglycemia
M. Hemostasis
Q. Aspirate

B. Complete blood count
F. Centrifuge
J. Pipet
N. Contamination
R. Macrophage

C. Catheter
G. Syringe
K. Cannula
O. Peritoneal dialysis
S. Leukocyte

D. Epithelium
H. Differential
L. HIV
P. Contusion

7. *Find the hidden words. The words have been placed horizontally, vertically, or diagonally. When you locate a word, draw a circle around it.*

Y	L	T	I	M	P	L	A	N	T	S	Z	C	S	J	C	D	S	X	M
P	Y	H	A	P	B	L	O	O	D	L	E	T	T	I	N	G	A	T	V
H	M	R	L	A	N	C	E	T	T	H	R	O	M	B	O	S	I	S	E
L	P	O	F	Z	S	E	M	I	P	E	R	M	E	A	B	L	E	Q	N
E	H	M	V	A	S	O	C	O	N	S	T	R	I	C	T	I	O	N	T
B	O	B	P	L	A	T	E	L	E	T	E	F	F	E	R	E	N	T	R
I	C	O	A	E	R	O	S	O	L	C	A	N	I	S	T	E	R	S	A
T	Y	C	A	P	E	R	I	P	H	E	R	A	L	B	L	O	O	D	L
I	T	Y	S	A	M	B	L	E	E	D	I	N	G	T	I	M	E	Q	H
S	E	T	M	L	Y	S	O	S	O	M	E	A	N	T	E	R	I	O	R
X	P	E	R	I	T	O	N	E	A	L	D	I	A	L	Y	S	I	S	X
A	P		C	I	R	C	U	L	A	T	O	R	Y	S	Y	S	T	E	M

1. Pertaining to the front side of the body.
2. A test which measures the time it takes for small blood vessels to close off and bleeding to stop.
3. Blood obtained from the circulation away from the heart, such as from the fingertip, heel pad, earlobe or from an antecubital vein.
4. Also known as a platelet, this is a particulate component of the blood, approximately 2-4 microns in diameter and known for its involvement in blood coagulation.
5. Also known as a thrombocyte, this is a particulate component of the blood known for its involvement in blood coagulation.
6. Permitting the passage of certain molecules and hindering others.
7. The formation of a blood clot (thrombus) within a vessel.
8. The circulatory system is composed of the heart, arteries, capillaries and veins.
9. Enclosed containers used to hold specimen tubes for centrifugation.
10. Toward the front or in front of.
11. A decrease in the inside diameter of especially arterioles leading to a decrease in blood flow to a part.
12. Dialysis through the peritoneum.
13. An object or material, such as tissue, partially or totally inserted or grafted into the body of a recipient.
14. The act or process of letting blood or bleeding, as by opening a vein or artery, or by cupping or leeches.
15. Carrying away. An artery is an efferent vessel carrying blood away from the heart.
16. One of the minute particles seen with the electron microscope in many types of cells, containing various hydrolytic enzymes and normally involved in the process of localized digestion inside the cell.
17. A small pointed blade usually with two edges used for incising or puncturing.
18. Any of the mononuclear, nonphagocytic leukocytes, found in the blood and lymph, which are the body's immunologically competent cells.
19. Inflammation of a vein. The condition is marked by infiltration of the layers of the vein and the formation of a clot. It produces edema, stiffness and pain in the affected area.

A. Thrombosis
B. Circulatory System
C. Aerosol canisters
D. Ventral
E. Peripheral blood
F. Bleeding time
G. Lancet
H. Lysosome
I. Bloodletting
J. Vasoconstriction
K. Anterior
L. Platelet
M. Semipermeable
N. Thrombocyte
O. Lymphocyte
P. Implant
Q. Peritoneal dialysis
R. Phlebitis
S. Efferent

8. *Find the hidden words. The words have been placed horizontally, vertically, or diagonally. When you locate a word, draw a circle around it.*

Z	P	G	N	F	L	R	S	E	M	I	P	E	R	M	E	A	B	L	E
E	A	X	Z	B	A	J	H	H	E	M	O	D	I	A	L	Y	S	I	S
U	M	C	O	N	T	A	C	T	P	R	E	C	A	U	T	I	O	N	S
V	D	V	V	T	E	Z	H	F	I	B	R	I	N	O	G	E	N	F	F
E	V	A	Y	Z	R	M	E	B	R	S	Y	R	I	N	G	E	P	V	M
B	O	C	S	H	A	F	M	R	E	D	B	L	O	O	D	C	E	L	L
M	K	U	I	O	L	E	A	A	L	L	E	R	G	E	N	C	R	Z	I
T	S	O	V	A	C	U	T	A	I	N	E	R	S	Y	S	T	E	M	D
M	B	L	O	O	D	B	O	R	N	E	P	A	T	H	O	G	E	N	S
I	B	E	D	A	J	T	M	H	Y	P	O	G	L	Y	C	E	M	I	A
K	K	P	G	F	C	I	A	H	D	A	R	T	E	R	Y	P	I	T	B
E	Q	E	C	C	H	Y	M	O	S	I	S	G	R	A	F	T	R	L	K

1. A localized collection of blood within tissue due to leakage from the wall of a blood vessel, producing a bluish discoloration (ecchymosis)and pain.
2. An instrument used to inject fluids into or aspirate fluids from any vessel or cavity.
3. Any small space of cavity formed in the protoplasm of a cell.
4. An abnormally low glucose level in the blood.
5. Blood vessel carrying blood away from the heart. Arterial blood is normally full of oxygen.
6. The skin discoloration caused by a bruise (contusion).
7. A position farther from the midline of the body or another reference structure.
8. The removal of certain components of the blood by diffusion through a semipermeable membrane.
9. This precaution is for specified patients known or suspected to be infected or colonized with microorganisms that can be transmitted by direct contact with the patient.
10. An implant or transplant of any tissue or organ.
11. Permitting the passage of certain molecules and hindering others.
12. The combination of a Vacutainer holder, needle and sample tube which allows for a more automated method of drawing blood.
13. A needle that attaches to a syringe for injections or withdrawal of fluids such as blood.
14. Precautions that are designed for the care of all patients in hospitals regardless of their diagnosis or presumed infection status.
15. The selective separation and removal of platelets from withdrawn blood. The remainder of the blood is re-transfused back into the donor.
16. Any disease producing microorganism which is spread through direct contact with contaminated blood.
17. The component of the blood that contains hemoglobin which is responsible for oxygen and carbon dioxide exchange.
18. An antigenic substance capable of producing an immediate-type hypersensitivity (allergy).
19. The protein from which fibrin is formed.

A. Contact Precautions
B. Standard Precautions
C. Hypoglycemia
D. Bloodborne pathogens
E. Graft
F. Semipermeable
G. Fibrinogen
H. Ecchymosis
I. Hemodialysis
J. Vacutainer System
K. Red blood cell
L. Hematoma
M. Vacuole
N. Hypodermic needle
O. Artery
P. Syringe
Q. Lateral
R. Plateletpheresis
S. Allergen

9. *Find the hidden words. The words have been placed horizontally, vertically, or diagonally. When you locate a word, draw a circle around it.*

K	B	D	H	M	V	W	S	Q	A	F	A	T	U	B	T	X	F	G	T
I	A	E	E	Y	E	X	Y	U	N	V	N	O	X	L	H	E	C	L	B
V	U	N	M	K	N	A	R	Z	A	A	E	U	H	O	R	A	Q	Z	L
V	R	Q	O	T	I	P	I	I	P	C	S	R	E	O	O	N	Q	X	O
O	Z	A	D	L	P	E	N	C	H	U	T	N	P	D	M	T	A	K	O
G	H	O	I	D	U	H	G	V	Y	O	H	I	A	L	B	E	U	H	D
H	Y	F	A	I	N	Z	E	M	L	L	E	Q	T	E	O	R	P	F	F
D	Y	K	L	P	C	D	P	K	A	E	T	U	I	T	C	I	W	I	I
Z	G	Y	Y	D	T	R	H	S	X	U	I	E	T	T	Y	O	D	D	L
T	L	N	S	R	U	A	X	J	I	L	C	T	I	I	T	R	R	C	M
H	Y	B	I	J	R	U	H	G	S	S	L	H	S	N	E	R	W	R	V
I	P	W	S	D	E	Q	V	O	L	A	R	R	A	G		N	O	V	I

1. An acute, generalized life-threatening allergic or hypersensitive reaction.
2. Also known as a platelet, this is a particulate component of the blood, approximately 2-4 microns in diameter and known for its involvement in blood coagulation.
3. A drug that causes unconsciousness or a loss of general sensation. A local anesthetic causes loss of feeling in a part of the body.
4. An instrument used to inject fluids into or aspirate fluids from any vessel or cavity.
5. The removal of certain components of the blood by diffusion through a semipermeable membrane.
6. The major human blood type system which depends on the presence or absence of antigens known as A and B.
7. A sample of blood is applied to a microscope slide and then studied under the microscope.
8. Usually a self-limited viral disease. Transmission is usually the result of poor hygiene and most often through the fecal-oral route.
9. A cylindrical shaped holder that accepts a Vacutainer tube on one end and a Vacutainer needle on the other.
10. A hollow silicone (soft, rubber-like material) tube inserted and secured into a large vein in the chest for long-term use to administer drugs or nutrients.
11. The hemoglobin compound bound with carbon dioxide in the red blood cells.
12. Toward the front or in front of.
13. The act or process of letting blood or bleeding, as by opening a vein or artery, or by cupping or leeches.
14. A method used by microbiologists and clinicians to keep cultures, sterile instruments and media, and people free of microbial contamination.
15. Pertaining to the palm or sole; indicating the flexor portion of the forearm, wrist or hand.
16. A constrictive band, placed over an extremity to distend veins for blood aspiration or intravenous injections.
17. The puncture of a vein for any purpose
18. Any small space of cavity formed in the protoplasm of a cell.

A. ABO Blood Group
E. Thrombocyte
I. Carbamate hemoglobin
M. Venipuncture
Q. Tourniquet
B. Aseptic technique
F. Syringe
J. Hickman catheter
N. Vacuole
R. Hepatitis A
C. Anaphylaxis
G. Blood film
K. Anesthetic
O. Anterior
D. Bloodletting
H. Hemodialysis
L. Volar
P. Vacutainer Holder

10. *Find the hidden words. The words have been placed horizontally, vertically, or diagonally. When you locate a word, draw a circle around it.*

C	H	E	L	A	T	E	A	B	L	O	O	D	L	E	T	T	I	N	G
E	V	B	U	Q	G	J	E	S	T	L	D	T	U	A	A	E	O	J	T
P	J	A	A	P	Z	J	R	W	M	Y	A	N	T	E	R	I	O	R	H
H	B	S	E	L	X	T	O	R	J	S	A	N	T	I	B	O	D	Y	R
A	L	I	T	A	K	B	B	F	U	O	T	H	R	O	M	B	U	S	O
L	O	L	I	T	Z	P	I	T	D	S	P	P	A	R	A	F	I	L	M
I	O	I	O	E	T	O	C	Z	Q	O	A	Z	I	T	P	N	L	N	B
C	D	C	L	L	C	X	U	H	K	M	L	I	T	G	R	R	Y	N	O
V	C	V	O	E	F	Z	W	Y	A	E	P	Y	X	Y	O	R	M	O	S
E	L	E	G	T	J	U	E	H	X	L	A	Z	J	S	N	B	P	Q	I
I	O	I	Y	P	L	A	S	M	A	Q	T	I	Z	V	E	V	H	X	S
N	T	N		B	Z	T	M	O	H	H	E	P	A	R	I	N		B	O

1. One of the minute particles seen with the electron microscope in many types of cells, containing various hydrolytic enzymes and normally involved in the process of localized digestion inside the cell.
2. Also known as a thrombocyte, this is a particulate component of the blood known for its involvement in blood coagulation.
3. A thin film of paraffin used primarily in the laboratory to seal open containers such as test tubes.
4. The fluid portion of the blood in which the cellular components are suspended. Plasma contains coagulation factors used in the clotting of blood as opposed to serum.
5. Having molecular oxygen present.
6. The conversion of blood from a liquid form to solid through the process of coagulation.
7. The act or process of letting blood or bleeding, as by opening a vein or artery, or by cupping or leeches.
8. Combining with a metallic ion into a ring complex.
9. The formation of a blood clot (thrombus) within a vessel.
10. Lying face down; opposed to supine.
11. A large vein of the arm that empties into the axillary vein

12. To examine or feel by the hand. In relation to venipunctures, this technique is used to "feel" a vein which will tend to rebound when slight pressure is applied with the finger.
13. The cause or origin of a disease or disorder.
14. A blood clot obstructing a blood vessel or a cavity of the heart. Heparin and Warfarin Sodium are being used to assist in dissolving or preventing clot formations.
15. Large vein on the inner side of the biceps. Often chosen for intravenous injections and blood drawing.
16. An anticoagulant that acts to inhibit coagulation factors, especially factor Xa. Heparin is formed in the liver.
17. Fluid found in lymphatic vessels and nodes derived from tissue fluids. Lymph is collected from all parts of the body and returned to the blood by the lymphatic system.
18. Toward the front or in front of.
19. A molecule that has a specific affinity for and reacts with the antigen that was responsible for its production or with one which is closely related.

A. Anterior
B. Lysosome
C. Chelate
D. Etiology
E. Basilic vein
F. Antibody
G. Thrombus
H. Aerobic
I. Prone
J. Platelet
K. Parafilm
L. Palpate
M. Heparin
N. Cephalic vein
O. Plasma
P. Lymph
Q. Blood clot
R. Thrombosis
S. Bloodletting

11. *Find the hidden words. The words have been placed horizontally, vertically, or diagonally. When you locate a word, draw a circle around it.*

D	W	Q	F	I	B	R	I	N	O	G	E	N	Y	R	B	J	C	Z	E
H	S	N	K	Z	I	J	N	P	B	A	S	I	L	I	C	V	E	I	N
W	H	E	P	A	T	I	T	I	S	B	P	E	M	B	O	L	U	S	Q
X	A	C	V	A	C	U	T	A	I	N	E	R	H	O	L	D	E	R	F
B	L	V	Z	X	B	U	M	D	S	T	H	E	M	A	T	O	M	A	O
J	B	V	E	N	U	L	E	K	M	O	N	O	N	U	C	L	E	A	R
P	U	A	Z	G	N	J	T	R	A	N	S	P	L	A	N	T	U	N	C
H	M	J	R	A	K	C	A	S	H	E	M	A	T	O	C	R	I	T	E
Y	I	M	Y	N	T	Q	G	K	E	T	I	O	L	O	G	Y		E	X
J	N	U	P	U	Q	K	B	L	O	O	D	C	O	U	N	T	Y	Y	M
P	P	B	H	H	E	P	A	T	I	T	I	S	C	L	Y	M	P	H	P
C	S	D	P	A	T	H	O	G	E	N	I	C	Y	N	Z	U	U	Y	U

1. An organ or tissue taken from the body for grafting into another part of the same body or into another individual.
2. A cylindrical shaped holder that accepts a Vacutainer tube on one end and a Vacutainer needle on the other.
3. A localized collection of blood within tissue due to leakage from the wall of a blood vessel, producing a bluish discoloration (ecchymosis)and pain.
4. The cause or origin of a disease or disorder.
5. A cell containing but one nucleus. In blood circulation, monocyte and lymphocyte.
6. Having the capability of producing disease.
7. The symbol used to depict the hydrogen ion concentration of a solution, i.e. acidity. pH 7.0 is neutral; above 7.0 is alkaline, below is acid.
8. A sudden blockage of a blood vessel by a blood clot or some other obstruction which has been transported through blood vessels and lodged at a site too small for passage.
9. An acute form of hepatitis caused by a virus. The virus is shed in body fluids of chronic and acute patients as well as asymptomatic carriers.
10. The determination of the proper number of red blood cells, white blood cells and platelets are present in the patient's blood.
11. Large vein on the inner side of the biceps. Often chosen for intravenous injections and blood drawing.
12. Main protein in human blood.
13. A very tiny vein, continuous with the capillaries. Compare with arteriole.
14. Inflammation of the liver.
15. Fluid found in lymphatic vessels and nodes derived from tissue fluids. Lymph is collected from all parts of the body and returned to the blood by the lymphatic system.
16. The protein from which fibrin is formed.
17. The ratio of the total red blood cell volume to the total blood volume and expressed as a percentage.
18. Enclosed containers used to hold specimen tubes for centrifugation.

A. Mononuclear
F. Etiology
K. Blood count
P. Vacutainer Holder

B. Pathogenic
G. Aerosol canisters
L. Hepatitis B
Q. Albumin

C. Hematocrit
H. Lymph
M. Transplant
R. Basilic vein

D. Venule
I. Fibrinogen
N. Hepatitis

E. Hematoma
J. Embolus
O. pH

12. *Find the hidden words. The words have been placed horizontally, vertically, or diagonally. When you locate a word, draw a circle around it.*

U	N	I	V	E	R	S	A	L	P	R	E	C	A	U	T	I	O	N	S
A	N	A	E	R	O	B	I	C	H	P	I	P	E	T	P	S	V	A	R
K	A	T	V	H	Y	P	O	G	L	Y	C	E	M	I	A	U	J	S	P
M	L	T	H	E	R	A	P	E	U	T	I	C	L	S	N	P	O	P	A
A	L	P	C	I	T	R	A	T	E	L	D	N	C	P	X	I	F	I	T
P	E	R	I	P	H	E	R	A	L	B	L	O	O	D	W	N	Y	R	H
R	R	B	L	O	O	D	C	O	U	N	T	Y	C	M	R	E	X	A	O
O	G	V	E	I	N	H	E	M	O	D	I	A	L	Y	S	I	S	T	G
A	E	R	A	S	E	P	T	I	C	T	E	C	H	N	I	Q	U	E	E
A	N	J	U	D	H	C	E	R	Y	T	H	R	O	C	Y	T	E	W	N
F	A	S	T	I	N	G	U	R	V	T	H	R	O	M	B	O	S	I	S
R	W	H	Y	P	E	R	S	E	N	S	I	T	I	V	I	T	Y		P

1. Blood obtained from the circulation away from the heart, such as from the fingertip, heel pad, earlobe or from an antecubital vein.
2. The removal of certain components of the blood by diffusion through a semipermeable membrane.
3. Cells that carry oxygen to all parts of the body.
4. Blood vessels carrying blood to the heart. Blood contained within these vessels is generally bound with carbon dioxide which will be exchanged for oxygen in the lungs.
5. A compound that is an intermediate in the citric acid cycle (Krebs cycle or glycolysis). Citrate chelates (binds) calcium ions, preventing blood clotting and, thus, is an effective anticoagulant.
6. A glass or transparent plastic tube used to accurately measure small amounts of liquid.
7. Pertaining to results obtained through treatment; having medicinal or healing properties; a healing agent.
8. An antigenic substance capable of producing an immediate-type hypersensitivity (allergy).
9. Growing, living or occurring in the absence of molecular oxygen; pertaining to an anaerobe.
10. An abnormally low glucose level in the blood.
11. As it relates to blood drawing, the material that is withdrawn with a negative pressure apparatus (syringe).
12. The determination of the proper number of red blood cells, white blood cells and platelets are present in the patient's blood.
13. A set of procedures and protocols designed to protect the healthcare worker which uses the basic concept that each patient must be treated as though they were infected with an infectious disease.
14. Lying down with the face up; opposed to prone.
15. A method used by microbiologists and clinicians to keep cultures, sterile instruments and media, and people free of microbial contamination.
16. A state in which the body reacts with an exaggerated immune response to a foreign substance. Reactions are classified as delayed or immediate types.
17. Without eating. Some laboratory tests are performed on "fasting" blood specimens such as sugar (glucose) levels and tolerance tests such as glucose, lactose and dextrose.
18. The formation of a blood clot (thrombus) within a vessel.
19. Any microorganism that produces disease.

A. Universal Precautions
B. Allergen
C. Aspirate
D. Hemodialysis
E. Supine
F. Peripheral blood
G. Thrombosis
H. Hypersensitivity
I. Citrate
J. Blood count
K. Fasting
L. Erythrocyte
M. Pathogen
N. Pipet
O. Therapeutic
P. Aseptic technique
Q. Vein
R. Hypoglycemia
S. Anaerobic

1. *Find the hidden words. The words have been placed horizontally, vertically, or diagonally. When you locate a word, draw a circle around it.*

A	A	N	A	E	R	O	B	I	C	K	A	S	P	I	R	A	T	E	Q
L	I	Z	W	A	R	F	A	R	I	N	S	O	D	I	U	M	D	P	T
Y	L	J	W	N	T	S	Q	I	E	X	K	S	M	V	D	V	M	A	N
T	I	F	I	S	T	U	L	A	Q	B	A	S	A	L	S	T	A	T	E
E	C	A	R	B	O	X	Y	H	E	M	O	G	L	O	B	I	N	H	B
S	L	A	M	I	N	A	R	F	L	O	W	H	O	O	D	O	C	O	H
E	R	Y	T	H	R	O	C	Y	T	E	H	U	M	O	R	A	L	G	X
E	Z	O	P	O	S	T	E	R	I	O	R	S	P	E	L	F	Y	E	N
K	D	S	A	D	V	A	S	C	U	L	A	R	G	R	A	F	T	N	P
F	A	S	T	I	N	G	U	T	O	U	R	N	I	Q	U	E	T	I	O
E	N	L	V	T	H	E	R	A	P	E	U	T	I	C	Z	W	P	C	D
U	R	M	V	A	C	U	T	A	I	N	E	R	H	O	L	D	E	R	S

1. An abnormal passageway usually between two internal organs. Such passages may be created experimentally for obtaining body secretions for study.
2. A type of an arteriovenous fistula consisting of either a venous autograft or synthetic tube which is grafted to the artery and vein.
3. Growing, living or occurring in the absence of molecular oxygen; pertaining to an anaerobe.
4. Situated at the back (dorsal) part of a structure.
5. The sodium salt of warfarin, one of the synthetic anticoagulants. Coumadin is a brand name.
6. Having the capability of producing disease.
7. The state of the body early in the morning, approximately 12 hours after the last ingestion of food or other nutrition.
8. Pertaining to elements dissolved in blood or body fluids, e.g., homoral immunity from antibodies in the blood as opposed to cellular immunity.
9. Hemoglobin which has been bound with carbon monoxide, which has an affinity for hemoglobin 200 times greater than oxygen.
10. Pertaining to results obtained through treatment; having medicinal or healing properties; a healing agent.

11. A constrictive band, placed over an extremity to distend veins for blood aspiration or intravenous injections.
12. A cylindrical shaped holder that accepts a Vacutainer tube on one end and a Vacutainer needle on the other.
13. Cells that carry oxygen to all parts of the body.
14. A substance that will acquire the capacity to conduct electricity when put into solution. Electrolytes include sodium, potassium, chloride, calcium and phosphate.
15. As it relates to blood drawing, the material that is withdrawn with a negative pressure apparatus (syringe).
16. Safety cabinets with air flow in such a direction as to carry any harmful materials or fumes away from the worker.
17. Without eating. Some laboratory tests are performed on "fasting" blood specimens such as sugar (glucose) levels and tolerance tests such as glucose, lactose and dextrose.

A. Aspirate
E. Therapeutic
I. Vascular graft
M. Basal state
Q. Anaerobic

B. Carboxyhemoglobin
F. Tourniquet
J. Fistula
N. Humoral

C. Lytes
G. Pathogenic
K. Vacutainer Holder
O. Erythrocyte

D. Laminar flow hood
H. Posterior
L. Fasting
P. Warfarin sodium

2. *Find the hidden words. The words have been placed horizontally, vertically, or diagonally. When you locate a word, draw a circle around it.*

W	H	P	P	O	T	B	P	P	T	A	Z	M	N	H	I	S	R	U	L
N	V	A	C	U	T	A	I	N	E	R	T	U	B	E	F	B	G	Y	
L	A	B	L	S	X	U	M	J	P	T	V	A	R	M	D	C	L	J	M
Y	T	L	Y	Y	T	G	Q	D	A	E	A	N	C	O	L	I	J	N	P
M	E	O	T	R	Y	K	O	Y	L	R	S	H	F	D	Q	T	D	X	H
P	J	O	E	I	H	M	L	L	M	I	C	W	A	I	V	R	J	U	O
H	C	D	S	N	F	T	J	M	A	O	U	D	I	A	A	A	K	F	C
E	T	C	H	G	S	P	D	S	R	L	L	B	N	L	C	T	V	N	Y
D	B	E	B	E	N	G	N	B	J	E	A	N	T	Y	U	E	F	C	T
E	B	L	G	H	V	T	T	S	Z	G	R	Q	D	S	O	S	U	Z	E
M	I	L	F	A	Y	G	L	U	C	O	S	E	I	L	O	T	Q	G	
A	R	Y	A	P	H	E	R	E	S	I	S	J	U	S	E	V	O	O	E

1. The removal of certain components of the blood by diffusion through a semipermeable membrane.
2. Blood sample tubes containing a vacuum. When the tube stopper is pierced by a Vacutainer needle which has been properly positioned in a vein, the vacuum draws blood into the tube.
3. The sugar measured in blood and urine specimens to determine the presence or absence of diabetes. Glucose is the product of carbohydrate metabolism and is the chief source of energy for all living organisms.
4. A type of swelling which occurs in lymphatic tissue when excess fluid collects in the arms or legs because the lymph nodes or vessels are blocked or removed.
5. There are three main types of cell in the blood stream. The red cell, which carries oxygen, the white cell, which fights infections and the platelet, which helps prevent bleeding.
6. Any small space of cavity formed in the protoplasm of a cell.
7. A small branch of an artery that leads to a capillary. Also, see capillary.
8. Referring to the palm surface or side of the hand
9. A substance that will acquire the capacity to conduct electricity when put into solution. Electrolytes include sodium, potassium, chloride, calcium and phosphate.
10. Hemoglobin which has been bound with carbon monoxide, which has an affinity for hemoglobin 200 times greater than oxygen.
11. A sudden loss of consciousness.
12. Pertaining to or composed of blood vessels. The vascular system is composed of the heart, blood vessels, lymphatics and their parts considered collectively.
13. A technique in which blood products are separated from a donor and the desired elements collected and the rest returned to the donor.
14. A cylindrical shaped holder that accepts a Vacutainer tube on one end and a Vacutainer needle on the other.
15. An instrument used to inject fluids into or aspirate fluids from any vessel or cavity.
16. The number of red blood cells, white blood cells and platelets (per cubic millimeter) that are present in the patient's sample of blood is determined.
17. A compound that is an intermediate in the citric acid cycle (Krebs cycle or glycolysis). Citrate chelates (binds) calcium ions, preventing blood clotting and, thus, is an effective anticoagulant.
18. Any of the mononuclear, nonphagocytic leukocytes, found in the blood and lymph, which are the body's immunologically competent cells.

A. Vacuole
E. Lymphocyte
I. Complete blood count
M. Arteriole
Q. Lytes

B. Glucose
F. Apheresis
J. Carboxyhemoglobin
N. Lymphedema
R. Vacutainer Holder

C. Faint
G. Hemodialysis
K. Vascular
O. Palmar

D. Citrate
H. Syringe
L. Blood cell
P. Vacutainer tube

3. *Find the hidden words. The words have been placed horizontally, vertically, or diagonally. When you locate a word, draw a circle around it.*

J	W	G	B	L	O	O	D	B	P	P	R	O	N	E	I	Y	S	L	M
Y	V	K	S	U	E	J	J	G	O	N	X	I	A	L	Z	M	T	L	U
P	J	L	Y	X	E	K	P	C	S	G	H	L	T	R	J	T	A	N	A
S	I	Y	M	M	O	A	L	O	T	E	F	F	L	U	E	N	T		I
Q	C	A	R	B	A	M	A	T	E	H	E	M	O	G	L	O	B	I	N
G	D	Y	W	U	P	N	T	I	R	G	L	U	C	O	S	E		C	B
Z	X	G	I	R	Y	B	E	X	I	N	C	O	N	T	U	S	I	O	N
W	S	U	P	I	N	E	L	N	O	O	M	K	G	D	N	I	D	U	K
K	P	N	E	Z	I	L	E	R	R	D	A	N	A	E	R	O	B	I	C
D	B	R	M	A	V	C	T	P	U	E	C	C	H	Y	M	O	S	I	S
O	N	D	A	L	C	R	Q	A	N	A	P	H	Y	L	A	X	I	S	N
P	O	V	I	D	O	N	E	I	O	D	I	N	E	Q	Q	C	F	F	H

1. The hemoglobin compound bound with carbon dioxide in the red blood cells.
2. The sugar measured in blood and urine specimens to determine the presence or absence of diabetes. Glucose is the product of carbohydrate metabolism and is the chief source of energy for all living organisms.
3. An outflow, usually of fluid.
4. Lying down with the face up; opposed to prone.
5. Situated at the back (dorsal) part of a structure.
6. Also known as a thrombocyte, this is a particulate component of the blood known for its involvement in blood coagulation.
7. The fluid in the body that contains red cells and white cells as well as platelets, proteins, plasma and other elements. It is transported throughout the body by the Circulatory System.
8. An acute, generalized life-threatening allergic or hypersensitive reaction.
9. Used as a topical antiseptic, this is a compound made by reacting iodine with povidone which slowly releases iodine.
10. Dialysis through the peritoneum.
11. Abbreviation for the Latin word statim, meaning immediately.
12. A decrease in the fluid content of the blood (plasma), resulting in an increase in concentration. This is determined by an increase in the hematocrit. Caused by a filtration of plasma into body tissues and often created by dehydration.
13. Growing, living or occurring in the absence of molecular oxygen; pertaining to an anaerobe.
14. A decrease in the inside diameter of especially arterioles leading to a decrease in blood flow to a part.
15. A bruise or injury without a break in the skin.
16. A hospital-borne infection. An infection whose origin is from within the hospital environment.
17. Lying face down; opposed to supine.
18. The skin discoloration caused by a bruise (contusion).
19. A type of coagulation (clotting) factors.

A. Effluent
E. Vasoconstriction
I. Contusion
M. Prone
Q. Anaphylaxis

B. Glucose
F. Peritoneal dialysis
J. Stat
N. Anaerobic
R. Platelet

C. Blood
G. Posterior
K. Antihemophilic factor
O. Ecchymosis
S. Povidone iodine

D. Hemoconcentration
H. Carbamate hemoglobin
L. Supine
P. Nosocomial infection

4. *Find the hidden words. The words have been placed horizontally, vertically, or diagonally. When you locate a word, draw a circle around it.*

Q	O	I	S	E	A	N	A	P	H	Y	L	A	X	I	S	S	P	B	C
Q	H	A	R	V	E	S	T	I	N	G	F	J	T	M	X	A	J	L	O
L	B	X	H	E	P	A	T	I	T	I	S	C	O	P	H	H	K	O	H
E	P	L	A	S	M	A	E	L	M	A	S	E	P	T	I	C	J	O	O
P	V	V	B	B	X	P	H	L	E	B	I	T	I	S	K	W	D	R	
I	M	M	J	P	O	V	I	D	O	N	E	I	O	D	I	N	E	V	T
D	H	Y	P	O	D	E	R	M	I	C	N	E	E	D	L	E	L	E	I
E	C	O	N	T	A	C	T	P	R	E	C	A	U	T	I	O	N	S	N
R	V	E	N	E	S	E	C	T	I	O	N	B	Y	W	Y	Q	R	S	G
M	P	A	L	P	A	T	E	P	U	Q	V	E	N	O	U	S	D	E	E
I	O	E	Q	P	Z	J	E	F	F	L	U	E	N	T		D	L	H	
S	S	T	A	N	D	A	R	D	P	R	E	C	A	U	T	I	O	N	S

1. Opening of a vein for collecting blood.
2. All the vessels lined with endothelium through which blood circulates.
3. Used as a topical antiseptic, this is a compound made by reacting iodine with povidone which slowly releases iodine.
4. In epidemiology, a group of individuals who share common characteristics.
5. The collection and preservation of tissues or cells from a donor for transplantation.
6. The most common form of hepatitis after blood transfusion. It is also the most prevalent form resulting from needle sharing by drug abusers.
7. The upper or outer layer of the two main layers of cells that make up the skin.
8. Precautions that are designed for the care of all patients in hospitals regardless of their diagnosis or presumed infection status.
9. Pertaining to the veins, or blood passing through them.
10. A set of procedures and protocols designed to protect the healthcare worker which uses the basic concept that each patient must be treated as though they were infected with an infectious disease.
11. This precaution is for specified patients known or suspected to be infected or colonized with microorganisms that can be transmitted by direct contact with the patient.
12. An outflow, usually of fluid.
13. Inflammation of a vein. The condition is marked by infiltration of the layers of the vein and the formation of a clot. It produces edema, stiffness and pain in the affected area.
14. The absence of microorganisms. By contrast, something that just discourages the growth of microorganisms is antiseptic.
15. The fluid portion of the blood in which the cellular components are suspended. Plasma contains coagulation factors used in the clotting of blood as opposed to serum.
16. An acute, generalized life-threatening allergic or hypersensitive reaction.
17. To examine or feel by the hand. In relation to venipunctures, this technique is used to "feel" a vein which will tend to rebound when slight pressure is applied with the finger.
18. A needle that attaches to a syringe for injections or withdrawal of fluids such as blood.

A. Cohorting
E. Blood vessel
I. Anaphylaxis
M. Epidermis
Q. Effluent

B. Palpate
F. Venous
J. Venesection
N. Povidone iodine
R. Contact Precautions

C. Hypodermic needle
G. Plasma
K. Universal Precautions
O. Harvesting

D. Hepatitis C
H. Aseptic
L. Standard Precautions
P. Phlebitis

5. *Find the hidden words. The words have been placed horizontally, vertically, or diagonally. When you locate a word, draw a circle around it.*

T	S	J	U	V	V	E	N	O	U	S	D	I	V	Q	M	D	X	Y	S
H	M	C	Y	T	O	P	L	A	S	M	C	H	R	O	M	A	T	I	N
E	N	Q	E	R	Y	T	H	R	O	C	Y	T	E	L	I	T	D	M	M
R	F	I	B	R	I	N	V	P	H	L	E	B	I	T	I	S	I	O	R
A	T	B	L	O	O	D	G	R	O	U	P	R	Q	N	X	A	A	N	H
P	G	V	E	N	U	L	E	A	S	E	P	T	I	C	K	E	L	O	M
E	I	J	B	T	S	E	B	U	I	V	Y	H	M	G	G	R	Y	C	W
U	S	D	Y	O	A	H	E	P	A	T	I	T	I	S	C	O	S	Y	K
T	Q	M	A	E	C	C	H	Y	M	O	S	I	S	Q	C	B	I	T	E
I	D	I	S	T	A	L	Q	K	O	K	B	R	O	P	Q	I	S	E	S
C	U	M	J	O	K	S	Y	N	C	O	P	E	Q	W	J	C	G	L	K
Q	F	E	H	W	L	Y	S	P	T	H	E	P	A	T	I	T	I	S	A

1. A very tiny vein, continuous with the capillaries. Compare with arteriole.
2. The process of cleansing the blood by passing it through a special machine. Dialysis is necessary when the kidneys are not able to filter the blood.
3. The liquid portion of a cell including organelles and inclusions suspended in it. It is the site of most chemical activities of the cell.
4. The skin discoloration caused by a bruise (contusion).
5. Remote, farther from any point of reference, opposed to proximal
6. Pertaining to results obtained through treatment; having medicinal or healing properties; a healing agent.
7. Usually a self-limited viral disease. Transmission is usually the result of poor hygiene and most often through the fecal-oral route.
8. Fainting; a temporary loss of consciousness due to a reduction of blood to the brain.
9. The protein formed during normal blood clotting that is the essence of the clot.
10. Pertaining to the veins, or blood passing through them.
11. A mononuclear, phagocytic leukocyte.
12. Inflammation of a vein. The condition is marked by infiltration of the layers of the vein and the formation of a clot. It produces edema, stiffness and pain in the affected area.
13. An inherited feature on the surface of the red blood cell. A series of related blood groups make up a blood group system such as the ABO system or the Rh system.
14. The most common form of hepatitis after blood transfusion. It is also the most prevalent form resulting from needle sharing by drug abusers.
15. Cells that carry oxygen to all parts of the body.
16. The more readily stainable portion of the cell nucleus. It is a DNA attached to a protein structure and is the carrier of genes in inheritance.
17. The absence of microorganisms. By contrast, something that just discourages the growth of microorganisms is antiseptic.
18. Having molecular oxygen present.

A. Therapeutic
B. Monocyte
C. Venule
D. Venous
E. Aerobic
F. Ecchymosis
G. Chromatin
H. Blood group
I. Fibrin
J. Aseptic
K. Syncope
L. Erythrocyte
M. Hepatitis A
N. Phlebitis
O. Hepatitis C
P. Dialysis
Q. Distal
R. Cytoplasm

6. *Find the hidden words. The words have been placed horizontally, vertically, or diagonally. When you locate a word, draw a circle around it.*

C	B	W	H	D	Y	H	O	F	E	P	I	T	H	E	L	I	U	M	C
H	C	C	E	L	V	C	O	N	T	A	M	I	N	A	T	I	O	N	O
I	E	A	M	E	R	Q	R	H	S	Y	S	T	E	M	F	Z	I	L	N
V	N	T	O	U	D	I	F	F	E	R	E	N	T	I	A	L	F	L	T
Z	T	H	S	K	A	S	P	I	R	A	T	E	A	P	Q	J	R	U	U
A	R	E	T	O	F	K	S	Y	R	I	N	G	E	P	I	P	E	T	S
C	I	T	A	C	F	F	Q	X	A	C	A	N	N	U	L	A	Z	S	I
L	F	E	S	Y	M	A	N	T	I	C	O	A	G	U	L	A	N	T	O
L	U	R	I	T	M	J	H	E	M	A	C	R	O	P	H	A	G	E	N
L	G	U	S	E	T	K	F	H	Y	P	O	G	L	Y	C	E	M	I	A
P	E	R	I	T	O	N	E	A	L	D	I	A	L	Y	S	I	S	V	W
C	O	M	P	L	E	T	E	B	L	O	O	D	C	O	U	N	T	R	Z

1. White blood cells.
2. An abnormally low glucose level in the blood.
3. Dialysis through the peritoneum.
4. A bruise or injury without a break in the skin.
5. The number of red blood cells, white blood cells and platelets (per cubic millimeter) that are present in the patient's sample of blood is determined.
6. An instrument used to inject fluids into or aspirate fluids from any vessel or cavity.
7. A thin, flexible tube. When a catheter is placed in a vein, it provides a pathway for giving drugs, nutrients, fluids, or blood products.
8. The soiling by inferior material, as by the introduction of organisms into a wound.
9. Human Immunodeficiency Virus
10. The most complex of all human blood groups and is responsible for serious hemolytic disease of the newborn.
11. A laboratory apparatus that separates mixed samples into homogenous component layers by spinning them at high speed.
12. A tube for insertion into a duct or cavity.
13. The outside layer of cells that covers all the free, open surfaces of the body including the skin, and mucous membranes that communicate with the outside of the body.
14. Any of the many forms of mononuclear phagocytes found in tissues and originating from stem cells in the bone marrow. In normal circulation, the monocyte may be categorized as a macrophage.
15. The cessation of bleeding, either by vasoconstriction and coagulation or by surgical means.
16. Any substance that prevents blood clotting.
17. A glass or transparent plastic tube used to accurately measure small amounts of liquid.
18. A count made on a stained blood smear of the proportion of the different leukocytes (WBC's) and expressed as a percentage.
19. As it relates to blood drawing, the material that is withdrawn with a negative pressure apparatus (syringe).

A. Anticoagulant
B. Complete blood count
C. Catheter
D. Epithelium
E. Rh System
F. Centrifuge
G. Syringe
H. Differential
I. Hypoglycemia
J. Pipet
K. Cannula
L. HIV
M. Hemostasis
N. Contamination
O. Peritoneal dialysis
P. Contusion
Q. Aspirate
R. Macrophage
S. Leukocyte

7. *Find the hidden words. The words have been placed horizontally, vertically, or diagonally. When you locate a word, draw a circle around it.*

Y	L	T	I	M	P	L	A	N	T	S	Z	C	S	J	C	D	S	X	M
P	Y	H	A	P	B	L	O	O	D	L	E	T	T	I	N	G	A	T	V
H	M	R	L	A	N	C	E	T	T	H	R	O	M	B	O	S	I	S	E
L	P	O	F	Z	S	E	M	I	P	E	R	M	E	A	B	L	E	Q	N
E	H	M	V	A	S	O	C	O	N	S	T	R	I	C	T	I	O	N	T
B	O	B	P	L	A	T	E	L	E	T	E	F	F	E	R	E	N	T	R
I	C	O	A	E	R	O	S	O	L	C	A	N	I	S	T	E	R	S	A
T	Y	C	A	P	E	R	I	P	H	E	R	A	L	B	L	O	O	D	L
I	T	Y	S	A	M	B	L	E	E	D	I	N	G	T	I	M	E	Q	H
S	E	T	M	L	Y	S	O	S	O	M	E	A	N	T	E	R	I	O	R
X	P	E	R	I	T	O	N	E	A	L	D	I	A	L	Y	S	I	S	X
A	P	C	I	R	C	U	L	A	T	O	R	Y	S	Y	S	T	E	M	

1. Pertaining to the front side of the body.
2. A test which measures the time it takes for small blood vessels to close off and bleeding to stop.
3. Blood obtained from the circulation away from the heart, such as from the fingertip, heel pad, earlobe or from an antecubital vein.
4. Also known as a platelet, this is a particulate component of the blood, approximately 2-4 microns in diameter and known for its involvement in blood coagulation.
5. Also known as a thrombocyte, this is a particulate component of the blood known for its involvement in blood coagulation.
6. Permitting the passage of certain molecules and hindering others.
7. The formation of a blood clot (thrombus) within a vessel.
8. The circulatory system is composed of the heart, arteries, capillaries and veins.
9. Enclosed containers used to hold specimen tubes for centrifugation.
10. Toward the front or in front of.
11. A decrease in the inside diameter of especially arterioles leading to a decrease in blood flow to a part.
12. Dialysis through the peritoneum.
13. An object or material, such as tissue, partially or totally inserted or grafted into the body of a recipient.
14. The act or process of letting blood or bleeding, as by opening a vein or artery, or by cupping or leeches.
15. Carrying away. An artery is an efferent vessel carrying blood away from the heart.
16. One of the minute particles seen with the electron microscope in many types of cells, containing various hydrolytic enzymes and normally involved in the process of localized digestion inside the cell.
17. A small pointed blade usually with two edges used for incising or puncturing.
18. Any of the mononuclear, nonphagocytic leukocytes, found in the blood and lymph, which are the body's immunologically competent cells.
19. Inflammation of a vein. The condition is marked by infiltration of the layers of the vein and the formation of a clot. It produces edema, stiffness and pain in the affected area.

A. Thrombosis
B. Circulatory System
C. Aerosol canisters
D. Ventral
E. Peripheral blood
F. Bleeding time
G. Lancet
H. Lysosome
I. Bloodletting
J. Vasoconstriction
K. Anterior
L. Platelet
M. Semipermeable
N. Thrombocyte
O. Lymphocyte
P. Implant
Q. Peritoneal dialysis
R. Phlebitis
S. Efferent

8. *Find the hidden words. The words have been placed horizontally, vertically, or diagonally. When you locate a word, draw a circle around it.*

Z	P	G	N	F	L	R	S	E	M	I	P	E	R	M	E	A	B	L	E
E	A	X	Z	B	A	J	H	H	E	M	O	D	I	A	L	Y	S	I	S
U	M	C	O	N	T	A	C	T	P	R	E	C	A	U	T	I	O	N	S
V	D	V	V	T	E	Z	H	F	I	B	R	I	N	O	G	E	N	F	F
E	V	A	Y	Z	R	M	E	B	R	S	Y	R	I	N	G	E	P	V	M
B	O	C	S	H	A	F	M	R	E	D	B	L	O	O	D	C	E	L	L
M	K	U	I	O	L	E	A	A	L	L	E	R	G	E	N	C	R	Z	I
T	S	O	V	A	C	U	T	A	I	N	E	R	S	Y	S	T	E	M	D
M	B	L	O	O	D	B	O	R	N	E	P	A	T	H	O	G	E	N	S
I	B	E	D	A	J	T	M	H	Y	P	O	G	L	Y	C	E	M	I	A
K	K	P	G	F	C	I	A	H	D	A	R	T	E	R	Y	P	I	T	B
E	Q	E	C	C	H	Y	M	O	S	I	S	G	R	A	F	T	R	L	K

1. A localized collection of blood within tissue due to leakage from the wall of a blood vessel, producing a bluish discoloration (ecchymosis)and pain.
2. An instrument used to inject fluids into or aspirate fluids from any vessel or cavity.
3. Any small space of cavity formed in the protoplasm of a cell.
4. An abnormally low glucose level in the blood.
5. Blood vessel carrying blood away from the heart. Arterial blood is normally full of oxygen.
6. The skin discoloration caused by a bruise (contusion).
7. A position farther from the midline of the body or another reference structure.
8. The removal of certain components of the blood by diffusion through a semipermeable membrane.
9. This precaution is for specified patients known or suspected to be infected or colonized with microorganisms that can be transmitted by direct contact with the patient.
10. An implant or transplant of any tissue or organ.
11. Permitting the passage of certain molecules and hindering others.
12. The combination of a Vacutainer holder, needle and sample tube which allows for a more automated method of drawing blood.
13. A needle that attaches to a syringe for injections or withdrawal of fluids such as blood.
14. Precautions that are designed for the care of all patients in hospitals regardless of their diagnosis or presumed infection status.
15. The selective separation and removal of platelets from withdrawn blood. The remainder of the blood is re-transfused back into the donor.
16. Any disease producing microorganism which is spread through direct contact with contaminated blood.
17. The component of the blood that contains hemoglobin which is responsible for oxygen and carbon dioxide exchange.
18. An antigenic substance capable of producing an immediate-type hypersensitivity (allergy).
19. The protein from which fibrin is formed.

A. Contact Precautions
E. Graft
I. Hemodialysis
M. Vacuole
Q. Lateral

B. Standard Precautions
F. Semipermeable
J. Vacutainer System
N. Hypodermic needle
R. Plateletpheresis

C. Hypoglycemia
G. Fibrinogen
K. Red blood cell
O. Artery
S. Allergen

D. Bloodborne pathogens
H. Ecchymosis
L. Hematoma
P. Syringe

9. *Find the hidden words. The words have been placed horizontally, vertically, or diagonally. When you locate a word, draw a circle around it.*

K	B	D	H	M	V	W	S	Q	A	F	A	T	U	B	T	X	F	G	T
I	A	E	E	Y	E	X	Y	U	N	V	N	O	X	L	H	E	C	L	B
V	U	N	M	K	N	A	R	Z	A	A	E	U	H	O	R	A	Q	Z	L
V	R	Q	O	T	I	P	I	I	P	C	S	R	E	O	O	N	Q	X	O
O	Z	A	D	L	P	E	N	C	H	U	T	N	P	D	M	T	A	K	O
G	H	O	I	D	U	H	G	V	Y	O	H	I	A	L	B	E	U	H	D
H	Y	F	A	I	N	Z	E	M	L	L	E	Q	T	E	O	R	P	F	F
D	Y	K	L	P	C	D	P	K	A	E	T	U	I	T	C	I	W	I	I
Z	G	Y	Y	D	T	R	H	S	X	U	I	E	T	T	Y	O	D	D	L
T	L	N	S	R	U	A	X	J	I	L	C	T	I	I	T	R	R	C	M
H	Y	B	I	J	R	U	H	G	S	S	L	H	S	N	E	R	W	R	V
I	P	W	S	D	E	Q	V	O	L	A	R	R	A	G	N	O	V	I

1. An acute, generalized life-threatening allergic or hypersensitive reaction.
2. Also known as a platelet, this is a particulate component of the blood, approximately 2-4 microns in diameter and known for its involvement in blood coagulation.
3. A drug that causes unconsciousness or a loss of general sensation. A local anesthetic causes loss of feeling in a part of the body.
4. An instrument used to inject fluids into or aspirate fluids from any vessel or cavity.
5. The removal of certain components of the blood by diffusion through a semipermeable membrane.
6. The major human blood type system which depends on the presence or absence of antigens known as A and B.
7. A sample of blood is applied to a microscope slide and then studied under the microscope.
8. Usually a self-limited viral disease. Transmission is usually the result of poor hygiene and most often through the fecal-oral route.
9. A cylindrical shaped holder that accepts a Vacutainer tube on one end and a Vacutainer needle on the other.
10. A hollow silicone (soft, rubber-like material) tube inserted and secured into a large vein in the chest for long-term use to administer drugs or nutrients.
11. The hemoglobin compound bound with carbon dioxide in the red blood cells.
12. Toward the front or in front of.
13. The act or process of letting blood or bleeding, as by opening a vein or artery, or by cupping or leeches.
14. A method used by microbiologists and clinicians to keep cultures, sterile instruments and media, and people free of microbial contamination.
15. Pertaining to the palm or sole; indicating the flexor portion of the forearm, wrist or hand.
16. A constrictive band, placed over an extremity to distend veins for blood aspiration or intravenous injections.
17. The puncture of a vein for any purpose
18. Any small space of cavity formed in the protoplasm of a cell.

A. ABO Blood Group
E. Thrombocyte
I. Carbamate hemoglobin
M. Venipuncture
Q. Tourniquet

B. Aseptic technique
F. Syringe
J. Hickman catheter
N. Vacuole
R. Hepatitis A

C. Anaphylaxis
G. Blood film
K. Anesthetic
O. Anterior

D. Bloodletting
H. Hemodialysis
L. Volar
P. Vacutainer Holder

10. *Find the hidden words. The words have been placed horizontally, vertically, or diagonally. When you locate a word, draw a circle around it.*

C	H	E	L	A	T	E	A	B	L	O	O	D	L	E	T	T	I	N	G
E	V	B	U	Q	G	J	E	S	T	L	D	T	U	A	A	E	O	J	T
P	J	A	A	P	Z	J	R	W	M	Y	A	N	T	E	R	I	O	R	H
H	B	S	E	L	X	T	O	R	J	S	A	N	T	I	B	O	D	Y	R
A	L	I	T	A	K	B	B	F	U	O	T	H	R	O	M	B	U	S	O
L	O	L	I	T	Z	P	I	T	D	S	P	P	A	R	A	F	I	L	M
I	O	I	O	E	T	O	C	Z	Q	O	A	Z	I	T	P	N	L	N	B
C	D	C	L	L	C	X	U	H	K	M	L	I	T	G	R	R	Y	N	O
V	C	V	O	E	F	Z	W	Y	A	E	P	Y	X	Y	O	R	M	O	S
E	L	E	G	T	J	U	E	H	X	L	A	Z	J	S	N	B	P	Q	I
I	O	I	Y	P	L	A	S	M	A	Q	T	I	Z	V	E	V	H	X	S
N	T	N	B	Z	T	M	O	H	H	E	P	A	R	I	N	B	O

1. One of the minute particles seen with the electron microscope in many types of cells, containing various hydrolytic enzymes and normally involved in the process of localized digestion inside the cell.
2. Also known as a thrombocyte, this is a particulate component of the blood known for its involvement in blood coagulation.
3. A thin film of paraffin used primarily in the laboratory to seal open containers such as test tubes.
4. The fluid portion of the blood in which the cellular components are suspended. Plasma contains coagulation factors used in the clotting of blood as opposed to serum.
5. Having molecular oxygen present.
6. The conversion of blood from a liquid form to solid through the process of coagulation.
7. The act or process of letting blood or bleeding, as by opening a vein or artery, or by cupping or leeches.
8. Combining with a metallic ion into a ring complex.
9. The formation of a blood clot (thrombus) within a vessel.
10. Lying face down; opposed to supine.
11. A large vein of the arm that empties into the axillary vein

12. To examine or feel by the hand. In relation to venipunctures, this technique is used to "feel" a vein which will tend to rebound when slight pressure is applied with the finger.
13. The cause or origin of a disease or disorder.
14. A blood clot obstructing a blood vessel or a cavity of the heart. Heparin and Warfarin Sodium are being used to assist in dissolving or preventing clot formations.
15. Large vein on the inner side of the biceps. Often chosen for intravenous injections and blood drawing.
16. An anticoagulant that acts to inhibit coagulation factors, especially factor Xa. Heparin is formed in the liver.
17. Fluid found in lymphatic vessels and nodes derived from tissue fluids. Lymph is collected from all parts of the body and returned to the blood by the lymphatic system.
18. Toward the front or in front of.
19. A molecule that has a specific affinity for and reacts with the antigen that was responsible for its production or with one which is closely related.

A. Anterior
B. Lysosome
C. Chelate
D. Etiology
E. Basilic vein
F. Antibody
G. Thrombus
H. Aerobic
I. Prone
J. Platelet
K. Parafilm
L. Palpate
M. Heparin
N. Cephalic vein
O. Plasma
P. Lymph
Q. Blood clot
R. Thrombosis
S. Bloodletting

11. *Find the hidden words. The words have been placed horizontally, vertically, or diagonally. When you locate a word, draw a circle around it.*

D	W	Q	F	I	B	R	I	N	O	G	E	N	Y	R	B	J	C	Z	E
H	S	N	K	Z	I	J	N	P	B	A	S	I	L	I	C	V	E	I	N
W	H	E	P	A	T	I	T	I	S	B	P	E	M	B	O	L	U	S	Q
X	A	C	V	A	C	U	T	A	I	N	E	R	H	O	L	D	E	R	F
B	L	V	Z	X	B	U	M	D	S	T	H	E	M	A	T	O	M	A	O
J	B	V	E	N	U	L	E	K	M	O	N	O	N	U	C	L	E	A	R
P	U	A	Z	G	N	J	T	R	A	N	S	P	L	A	N	T	U	N	C
H	M	J	R	A	K	C	A	S	H	E	M	A	T	O	C	R	I	T	E
Y	I	M	Y	N	T	Q	G	K	E	T	I	O	L	O	G	Y		E	X
J	N	U	P	U	Q	K	B	L	O	O	D	C	O	U	N	T	Y	Y	M
P	P	B	H	H	E	P	A	T	I	T	I	S	C	L	Y	M	P	H	P
C	S	D	P	A	T	H	O	G	E	N	I	C	Y	N	Z	U	U	Y	U

1. An organ or tissue taken from the body for grafting into another part of the same body or into another individual.
2. A cylindrical shaped holder that accepts a Vacutainer tube on one end and a Vacutainer needle on the other.
3. A localized collection of blood within tissue due to leakage from the wall of a blood vessel, producing a bluish discoloration (ecchymosis)and pain.
4. The cause or origin of a disease or disorder.
5. A cell containing but one nucleus. In blood circulation, monocyte and lymphocyte.
6. Having the capability of producing disease.
7. The symbol used to depict the hydrogen ion concentration of a solution, i.e. acidity. pH 7.0 is neutral; above 7.0 is alkaline, below is acid.
8. A sudden blockage of a blood vessel by a blood clot or some other obstruction which has been transported through blood vessels and lodged at a site too small for passage.
9. An acute form of hepatitis caused by a virus. The virus is shed in body fluids of chronic and acute patients as well as asymptomatic carriers.
10. The determination of the proper number of red blood cells, white blood cells and platelets are present in the patient's blood.
11. Large vein on the inner side of the biceps. Often chosen for intravenous injections and blood drawing.
12. Main protein in human blood.
13. A very tiny vein, continuous with the capillaries. Compare with arteriole.
14. Inflammation of the liver.
15. Fluid found in lymphatic vessels and nodes derived from tissue fluids. Lymph is collected from all parts of the body and returned to the blood by the lymphatic system.
16. The protein from which fibrin is formed.
17. The ratio of the total red blood cell volume to the total blood volume and expressed as a percentage.
18. Enclosed containers used to hold specimen tubes for centrifugation.

A. Mononuclear
F. Etiology
K. Blood count
P. Vacutainer Holder

B. Pathogenic
G. Aerosol canisters
L. Hepatitis B
Q. Albumin

C. Hematocrit
H. Lymph
M. Transplant
R. Basilic vein

D. Venule
I. Fibrinogen
N. Hepatitis

E. Hematoma
J. Embolus
O. pH

12. *Find the hidden words. The words have been placed horizontally, vertically, or diagonally. When you locate a word, draw a circle around it.*

U	N	I	V	E	R	S	A	L	P	R	E	C	A	U	T	I	O	N	S
A	N	A	E	R	O	B	I	C	H	P	I	P	E	T	P	S	V	A	R
K	A	T	V	H	Y	P	O	G	L	Y	C	E	M	I	A	U	J	S	P
M	L	T	H	E	R	A	P	E	U	T	I	C	L	S	N	P	O	P	A
A	L	P	C	I	T	R	A	T	E	L	D	N	C	P	X	I	F	I	T
P	E	R	I	P	H	E	R	A	L	B	L	O	O	D	W	N	Y	R	H
R	R	B	L	O	O	D	C	O	U	N	T	Y	C	M	R	E	X	A	O
O	G	V	E	I	N	H	E	M	O	D	I	A	L	Y	S	I	S	T	G
A	E	R	A	S	E	P	T	I	C	T	E	C	H	N	I	Q	U	E	E
A	N	J	U	D	H	C	E	R	Y	T	H	R	O	C	Y	T	E	W	N
F	A	S	T	I	N	G	U	R	V	T	H	R	O	M	B	O	S	I	S
R	W	H	Y	P	E	R	S	E	N	S	I	T	I	V	I	T	Y		P

1. Blood obtained from the circulation away from the heart, such as from the fingertip, heel pad, earlobe or from an antecubital vein.
2. The removal of certain components of the blood by diffusion through a semipermeable membrane.
3. Cells that carry oxygen to all parts of the body.
4. Blood vessels carrying blood to the heart. Blood contained within these vessels is generally bound with carbon dioxide which will be exchanged for oxygen in the lungs.
5. A compound that is an intermediate in the citric acid cycle (Krebs cycle or glycolysis). Citrate chelates (binds) calcium ions, preventing blood clotting and, thus, is an effective anticoagulant.
6. A glass or transparent plastic tube used to accurately measure small amounts of liquid.
7. Pertaining to results obtained through treatment; having medicinal or healing properties; a healing agent.
8. An antigenic substance capable of producing an immediate-type hypersensitivity (allergy).
9. Growing, living or occurring in the absence of molecular oxygen; pertaining to an anaerobe.
10. An abnormally low glucose level in the blood.
11. As it relates to blood drawing, the material that is withdrawn with a negative pressure apparatus (syringe).
12. The determination of the proper number of red blood cells, white blood cells and platelets are present in the patient's blood.
13. A set of procedures and protocols designed to protect the healthcare worker which uses the basic concept that each patient must be treated as though they were infected with an infectious disease.
14. Lying down with the face up; opposed to prone.
15. A method used by microbiologists and clinicians to keep cultures, sterile instruments and media, and people free of microbial contamination.
16. A state in which the body reacts with an exaggerated immune response to a foreign substance. Reactions are classified as delayed or immediate types.
17. Without eating. Some laboratory tests are performed on "fasting" blood specimens such as sugar (glucose) levels and tolerance tests such as glucose, lactose and dextrose.
18. The formation of a blood clot (thrombus) within a vessel.
19. Any microorganism that produces disease.

A. Universal Precautions
B. Allergen
C. Aspirate
D. Hemodialysis
E. Supine
F. Peripheral blood
G. Thrombosis
H. Hypersensitivity
I. Citrate
J. Blood count
K. Fasting
L. Erythrocyte
M. Pathogen
N. Pipet
O. Therapeutic
P. Aseptic technique
Q. Vein
R. Hypoglycemia
S. Anaerobic

Glossary

ABO Blood Group: The major human blood type system which depends on the presence or absence of antigens known as A and B.

Absorb: To suck up, as through pores.

Acute: Of short duration. Rapid and abbreviated in onset.

Adsorb: To attract and retain other material on the surface.

Aerobic: Having molecular oxygen present.

Aerosol canisters: Enclosed containers used to hold specimen tubes for centrifugation.

Albumin: Main protein in human blood.

Allergen: An antigenic substance capable of producing an immediate-type hypersensitivity (allergy).

Anaerobic: Growing, living or occurring in the absence of molecular oxygen; pertaining to an anaerobe.

Anaphylaxis: An acute, generalized life-threatening allergic or hypersensitive reaction.

Anemia: The condition of having less than the normal number of red blood cells or hemoglobin in the blood.

Anesthetic: A drug that causes unconsciousness or a loss of general sensation. A local anesthetic causes loss of feeling in a part of the body.

Antecubital fossa: That part of the arm opposing the elbow.

Anterior: Toward the front or in front of.

Antibody: A molecule that has a specific affinity for and reacts with the antigen that was responsible for its production or with one which is closely related.

Anticoagulant: Any substance that prevents blood clotting.

Antigen   : A substance capable of producing a specific immune response with a specific antibody.

Antihemophilic factor: A type of coagulation (clotting) factors.

Antiplatelet agent: Medications that, like aspirin, reduce the tendency of platelets in the blood to clump and clot.

Antiseptic: Something that discourages the growth microorganisms. By contrast, aseptic refers to the absence of microorganisms.

Apheresis: A technique in which blood products are separated from a donor and the desired elements collected and the rest returned to the donor.

Arteriole: A small branch of an artery that leads to a capillary. Also, see capillary.

Arteriovenous fistula: The surgical joining of an artery and a vein under the skin for hemodialysis.

Artery: Blood vessel carrying blood away from the heart. Arterial blood is normally full of oxygen.

Aseptic: The absence of microorganisms. By contrast, something that just discourages the growth of microorganisms is antiseptic.

Aseptic technique: A method used by microbiologists and clinicians to keep cultures, sterile instruments and media, and people free of microbial contamination.

Aspirate: As it relates to blood drawing, the material that is withdrawn with a negative pressure apparatus (syringe).

Autohemolysis: Hemolysis of red blood cells of a person by his own serum.

Bacteremia: The presence of viable bacteria circulating in the bloodstream. Diagnosed with blood cultures.

Basal state: The state of the body early in the morning, approximately 12 hours after the last ingestion of food or other nutrition.

Basilic vein: Large vein on the inner side of the biceps. Often chosen for intravenous injections and blood drawing.

Basophil: A granular leukocyte with an irregularly shaped nucleus that is partially constricted into two lobes, and with cytoplasm that contains coarse, bluish-black granules of variable size.

Betadine: A popular tradename iodine-containing topical antiseptic agent; povidone-iodine.

Bleeding time: A test which measures the time it takes for small blood vessels to close off and bleeding to stop.

Blind stick: Performing a venipuncture with no apparently visible or palpable vein.

Blood: The fluid in the body that contains red cells and white cells as well as platelets, proteins, plasma and other elements. It is transported throughout the body by the Circulatory System.

Bloodborne pathogens: Any disease producing microorganism which is spread through direct contact with contaminated blood.

Blood cell: There are three main types of cell in the blood stream. The red cell, which carries oxygen, the white cell, which fights infections and the platelet, which helps prevent bleeding.

Blood clot: The conversion of blood from a liquid form to solid through the process of coagulation.

Blood clotting factor: Any different protein factors which, when acting together, can form a blood clot shortly after platelets have broken at the site of the wound.

Blood count: The determination of the proper number of red blood cells, white blood cells and platelets are present in the patient's blood.

Blood culture: A test which involves the incubation of a blood specimen overnight to determine if bacteria are present.

Blood film: A sample of blood is applied to a microscope slide and then studied under the microscope.

Blood group: An inherited feature on the surface of the red blood cell. A series of related blood groups make up a blood group system such as the ABO system or the Rh system.

Bloodletting: The act or process of letting blood or bleeding, as by opening a vein or artery, or by cupping or leeches.

Blood smear: A sample of blood is applied to a microscope slide and then studied under the microscope.

Blood transfer device: A safety device designed to transfer blood from one container into another.

Blood vessel: All the vessels lined with endothelium through which blood circulates.

Bruise: A bruise or ""contusion" is a traumatic injury of the soft tissues which results in breakage of the local capillaries and leakage of red blood cells.

Butterfly: A small needle with two plastic wings attached which are squeezed together to form a tab that is used to manipulate the needle.

Cannula: A tube for insertion into a duct or cavity.

Capillary: Any one of the minute vessels that connect the arterioles and venules, forming a network in nearly all parts of the body.

Carbamate hemoglobin: The hemoglobin compound bound with carbon dioxide in the red blood cells.

Carboxyhemoglobin: Hemoglobin which has been bound with carbon monoxide, which has an affinity for hemoglobin 200 times greater than oxygen.

Catheter: A thin, flexible tube. When a catheter is placed in a vein, it provides a pathway for giving drugs, nutrients, fluids, or blood products.

Central venous catheter: Small, flexible plastic tube inserted into the large vein above the heart, through which drugs and blood products can be given and blood samples withdrawn painlessly.

Centrifuge: A laboratory apparatus that separates mixed samples into homogenous component layers by spinning them at high speed.

Cephalic vein: A large vein of the arm that empties into the axillary vein

Chelate: Combining with a metallic ion into a ring complex.

Chromatin: The more readily stainable portion of the cell nucleus. It is a DNA attached to a protein structure and is the carrier of genes in inheritance.

Circulation: The movement of fluid in a regular or circuitous course.

Circulatory System: The circulatory system is composed of the heart, arteries, capillaries and veins.

Citrate: A compound that is an intermediate in the citric acid cycle (Krebs cycle or glycolysis). Citrate chelates (binds) calcium ions, preventing blood clotting and, thus, is an effective anticoagulant.

Citrate phosphate dextrose: An anticoagulant.

Citric Acid Cycle   : A group or series of enzymatic reactions in living aerobic organisms that results in the production of energy.

Clot: A semisolid mass of blood found inside or outside the body.

Coagulate: The process of clot formation. Part of an important host defense mechanism call hemostasis.

Coagulation factors: Group of plasma protein substances (Factor I thru XIII) contained in the plasma, which act together to bring about blood coagulation.

Cohorting: In epidemiology, a group of individuals who share common characteristics.

Collateral circulation: Blood which infuses an area through a secondary or accessory route.

Complete blood count: The number of red blood cells, white blood cells and platelets (per cubic millimeter) that are present in the patient's sample of blood is determined.

Contact Precautions: This precaution is for specified patients known or suspected to be infected or colonized with microorganisms that can be transmitted by direct contact with the patient.

Contagious: Infectious. May be transmitted from person to person.

Contamination: The soiling by inferior material, as by the introduction of organisms into a wound.

Contusion: A bruise or injury without a break in the skin.

Coumadin: A brand name for warfarin sodium.

Cytoplasm: The liquid portion of a cell including organelles and inclusions suspended in it. It is the site of most chemical activities of the cell.

Cefibrinated blood: Blood which has been deprived of fibrin.

Dialysis: The process of cleansing the blood by passing it through a special machine. Dialysis is necessary when the kidneys are not able to filter the blood.

Diaphoretic: Formation of profuse perspiration (sweat). A symptom of syncope or vasovagal response.

Differential: A count made on a stained blood smear of the proportion of the different leukocytes (WBC's) and expressed as a percentage.

Disinfectant: An agent that disinfects, applied particularly to agents used on inanimate objects.

Distal: Remote, farther from any point of reference, opposed to proximal

Dorsal: Denoting a position more toward the back surface than some other object of reference; same as posterior in human anatomy.

Ecchymosis: The skin discoloration caused by a bruise (contusion).

Edema: The swelling of soft tissues caused by excess fluid accumulation.

EDTA: A calcium chelating (binding) agent that is used as an anticoagulant for laboratory blood specimens. Also used in treatment of lead poisoning.

Efferent: Carrying away. An artery is an efferent vessel carrying blood away from the heart.

Effluent   : An outflow, usually of fluid.

Electrolyte: A substance that will acquire the capacity to conduct electricity when put into solution.

Embolus: A sudden blockage of a blood vessel by a blood clot or some other obstruction which has been transported through blood vessels and lodged at a site too small for passage.

Endothelium: The layer of cells lining the closed internal spaces of the body such as the blood vessels and lymphatic vessels.

Engineering control: Controls (e.g., sharps disposal containers, self-sheathing needles) that isolate or remove the bloodborne pathogens hazard from the workplace.

Eosinophil: An eosin (red) staining leukocyte with a nucleus that usually has two lobes connected by a slender thread of chromatin, and cytoplasm containing coarse, round granules that are uniform in size.

Epidemiology: The science concerned with the study of factors influencing the distribution of disease and their causes in a defined population.

Epidermis: The upper or outer layer of the two main layers of cells that make up the skin.

Epithelium: The outside layer of cells that covers all the free, open surfaces of the body including the skin, and mucous membranes that communicate with the outside of the body.

Erythrocyte: Cells that carry oxygen to all parts of the body.

Etiology : The cause or origin of a disease or disorder.

Faint: A sudden loss of consciousness.

Fasting: Without eating. Some laboratory tests are performed on "fasting" blood specimens such as sugar (glucose) levels and tolerance tests such as glucose, lactose and dextrose.

Fibrin: The protein formed during normal blood clotting that is the essence of the clot.

Fibrinogen: The protein from which fibrin is formed.

Fistula: An abnormal passageway usually between two internal organs. Such passages may be created experimentally for obtaining body secretions for study.

Flash back: Relative to venipunctures, the appearance of a small amount of blood in the neck of a syringe or the tubing of a butterfly. This is a sign that the vein has been properly accessed.

Flexion: The process of bending or the state of being bent. Flexion of the fingers results in a clenched fist.

Gauge: Needle diameter is measured by gauge; the larger the needle diameter, the smaller the gauge.

Germicide: An agent that kills pathogenic microorganisms

Glucose : The sugar measured in blood and urine specimens to determine the presence or absence of diabetes. Glucose is the product of carbohydrate metabolism and is the chief source of energy for all living organisms.

Graft: An implant or transplant of any tissue or organ.

Harvesting: The collection and preservation of tissues or cells from a donor for transplantation.

Hematocrit: The ratio of the total red blood cell volume to the total blood volume and expressed as a percentage.

Hematoma: A localized collection of blood within tissue due to leakage from the wall of a blood vessel, producing a bluish discoloration (ecchymosis)and pain.

Hemoconcentration: A decrease in the fluid content of the blood (plasma), resulting in an increase in concentration. This is determined by an increase in the hematocrit. Caused by a filtration of plasma into body tissues and often created by dehydration.

Hemodialysis: The removal of certain components of the blood by diffusion through a semipermeable membrane.

Hemoglobin: The oxygen carrying pigment of the red blood cells.

Hemolysis: The breaking of the red blood cells membrane releasing free hemoglobin into the circulating blood.

Hemostasis: The cessation of bleeding, either by vasoconstriction and coagulation or by surgical means.

Heparin: An anticoagulant that acts to inhibit coagulation factors, especially factor Xa. Heparin is formed in the liver.

Hepatitis: Inflammation of the liver.

Hepatitis A: Usually a self-limited viral disease. Transmission is usually the result of poor hygiene and most often through the fecal-oral route.

Hepatitis B: An acute form of hepatitis caused by a virus. The virus is shed in body fluids of chronic and acute patients as well as asymptomatic carriers.

Hepatitis C: The most common form of hepatitis after blood transfusion. It is also the most prevalent form resulting from needle sharing by drug abusers.

Hickman catheter: A hollow silicone (soft, rubber-like material) tube inserted and secured into a large vein in the chest for long-term use to administer drugs or nutrients.

HIV: Human Immunodeficiency Virus

Humoral: Pertaining to elements dissolved in blood or body fluids, e.g., homoral immunity from antibodies in the blood as opposed to cellular immunity.

Hypersensitivity: A state in which the body reacts with an exaggerated immune response to a foreign substance. Reactions are classified as delayed or immediate types.

Hypodermic needle: A needle that attaches to a syringe for injections or withdrawal of fluids such as blood.

Hypoglycemia: An abnormally low glucose level in the blood.

Implant: An object or material, such as tissue, partially or totally inserted or grafted into the body of a recipient.

Invitro: Outside the living body; inside a glass; observable in a test tube.

Invivo: Inside the living body.

Laminar flow hood: Safety cabinets with air flow in such a direction as to carry any harmful materials or fumes away from the worker.

Lancet: A small pointed blade usually with two edges used for incising or puncturing.

Lateral: A position farther from the midline of the body or another reference structure.

Leukocyte: White blood cells.

Lymph: Fluid found in lymphatic vessels and nodes derived from tissue fluids. Lymph is collected from all parts of the body and returned to the blood by the lymphatic system.

Lymphedema: A type of swelling which occurs in lymphatic tissue when excess fluid collects in the arms or legs because the lymph nodes or vessels are blocked or removed.

Lymphocyte: Any of the mononuclear, nonphagocytic leukocytes, found in the blood and lymph, which are the body's immunologically competent cells.

Lysosome: One of the minute particles seen with the electron microscope in many types of cells, containing various hydrolytic enzymes and normally involved in the process of localized digestion inside the cell.

Lytes: A substance that will acquire the capacity to conduct electricity when put into solution. Electrolytes include sodium, potassium, chloride, calcium and phosphate.

Macrophage: Any of the many forms of mononuclear phagocytes found in tissues and originating from stem cells in the bone marrow. In normal circulation, the monocyte may be categorized as a macrophage.

Mean Corpuscular Volume: Average volume of red blood cells.

Medial: Pertaining to the middle aspect; closer to the midline of the body or structure.

Medial cubital vein: The forearm vein most commonly used for venipuncture because it is generally the largest and best-anchored vein

Microcapillary: Referring to collection of blood specimens by puncturing capillaries, usually in the heel of infants or the fingers of children and adults.

Monocyte: A mononuclear, phagocytic leukocyte.

Mononuclear: A cell containing but one nucleus. In blood circulation, monocyte and lymphocyte.

Multi sample adapter: A device used with a butterfly and Vacutainer holder to allow for the withdrawal of multiple tubes of blood during a venipuncture

Nosocomial infection: A hospital-borne infection. An infection whose origin is from within the hospital environment.

Order of Draw: Terminology used to define the order in which blood sample tubes should be drawn using a multi-sample technique such as the Vacutainer System.

Pallor: Paleness; decrease of absence of skin color.

Palmar: Referring to the palm surface or side of the hand

Palpate: To examine or feel by the hand. In relation to venipunctures, this technique is used to "feel" a vein which will tend to rebound when slight pressure is applied with the finger.

Parafilm: A thin film of paraffin used primarily in the laboratory to seal open containers such as test tubes.

Pathogen: Any microorganism that produces disease.

Pathogenic: Having the capability of producing disease.

Peripheral blood: Blood obtained from the circulation away from the heart, such as from the fingertip, heel pad, earlobe or from an antecubital vein.

Peritoneal dialysis: Dialysis through the peritoneum.

Peritoneum: The membrane lining the abdominal and pelvic wall.

pH: The symbol used to depict the hydrogen ion concentration of a solution, i.e. acidity. pH 7.0 is neutral; above 7.0 is alkaline, below is acid.

Phagocytosis: A process where polymorphonuclear leukocytes, monocytes, and macrophages combine with lysosomes within the cell cytoplasm to digest and destroy a particulate.

Phlebitis: Inflammation of a vein. The condition is marked by infiltration of the layers of the vein and the formation of a clot. It produces edema, stiffness and pain in the affected area.

Phlebotomist: One who practices phlebotomy.

Phlebotomy: The incision of a vein as for blood-letting (venesection); needle puncture of a vein for drawing blood (venipuncture).

Pipet: A glass or transparent plastic tube used to accurately measure small amounts of liquid.

Plasma: The fluid portion of the blood in which the cellular components are suspended. Plasma contains coagulation factors used in the clotting of blood as opposed to serum.

Platelet: Also known as a thrombocyte, this is a particulate component of the blood known for its involvement in blood coagulation.

Plateletpheresis: The selective separation and removal of platelets from withdrawn blood. The remainder of the blood is re-transfused back into the donor.

Posterior: Situated at the back (dorsal) part of a structure.

Povidone iodine: Used as a topical antiseptic, this is a compound made by reacting iodine with povidone which slowly releases iodine.

Prone: Lying face down; opposed to supine.

Prophylaxis: A preventative treatment.

Protoplasm: The viscid, translucent fluid that makes up the essential material of all plant and animal cells.

Proximal: Nearest to any other point of reference.

Red blood cell: The component of the blood that contains hemoglobin which is responsible for oxygen and carbon dioxide exchange.

Reverse isolation: An isolation procedure designed to protect the patient from contracting disease. Frequently used for transplant patients or for patients whose immune response has been greatly reduced.

Rh System: The most complex of all human blood groups and is responsible for serious hemolytic disease of the newborn.

Sclerosis: A hardening, especially from inflammation and certain disease states. Though sclerosis may occur in many areas of the body, the term is most often associated with blood vessels.

Semipermeable: Permitting the passage of certain molecules and hindering others.

Serum: Referring to blood, the clear liquid portion of blood that separates out after clotting has taken place. Since clotting has occurred, serum is fibrinogen deficient. Contrast to plasma.

Standard Precautions: Precautions that are designed for the care of all patients in hospitals regardless of their diagnosis or presumed infection status.

Stat: Abbreviation for the Latin word statim, meaning immediately.

Supine: Lying down with the face up; opposed to prone.

Syncope: Fainting; a temporary loss of consciousness due to a reduction of blood to the brain.

Syringe: An instrument used to inject fluids into or aspirate fluids from any vessel or cavity.

Therapeutic: Pertaining to results obtained through treatment; having medicinal or healing properties; a healing agent.

Thrombocyte   Also known as a platelet, this is a particulate component of the blood, approximately 2-4 microns in diameter and known for its involvement in blood coagulation.

Thrombocytopenia: Decrease in the number of blood platelets below normal values.

Thrombosis: The formation of a blood clot (thrombus) within a vessel.

Thrombus: A blood clot obstructing a blood vessel or a cavity of the heart. Heparin and Warfarin Sodium are being used to assist in dissolving or preventing clot formations.

Tourniquet: A constrictive band, placed over an extremity to distend veins for blood aspiration or intravenous injections.

Transmission Based Precautions: A category used for patients known or suspected to be infected or colonized with important pathogens.

Transplant: An organ or tissue taken from the body for grafting into another part of the same body or into another individual.

Universal Precautions: A set of procedures and protocols designed to protect the healthcare worker which uses the basic concept that each patient must be treated as though they were infected with an infectious disease.

Vacuole: Any small space of cavity formed in the protoplasm of a cell.

Vacutainer: A trade name now a generic term used to describe equipment used to automatically aspirate blood from a vessel by venipuncture.

Vacutainer Holder: A cylindrical shaped holder that accepts a Vacutainer tube on one end and a Vacutainer needle on the other.

Vacutainer System: The combination of a Vacutainer holder, needle and sample tube which allows for a more automated method of drawing blood.

Vacutainer tube   : Blood sample tubes containing a vacuum. When the tube stopper is pierced by a Vacutainer needle which has been properly positioned in a vein, the vacuum draws blood into the tube.

Vascular: Pertaining to or composed of blood vessels. The vascular system is composed of the heart, blood vessels, lymphatics and their parts considered collectively.

Vascular graft: A type of an arteriovenous fistula consisting of either a venous autograft or synthetic tube which is grafted to the artery and vein.

Vasoconstriction: A decrease in the inside diameter of especially arterioles leading to a decrease in blood flow to a part.

Vasovagal response: A transient vascular and neurogenic reaction marked by pallor, nausea, sweating, slowing heart rate and a rapid fall in arterial blood pressure which may result in loss of consciousness.

Vein: Blood vessels carrying blood to the heart. Blood contained within these vessels is generally bound with carbon dioxide which will be exchanged for oxygen in the lungs.

Venesection: Opening of a vein for collecting blood.

Venipuncture: The puncture of a vein for any purpose

Venous: Pertaining to the veins, or blood passing through them.

Ventral: Pertaining to the front side of the body.

Venule: A very tiny vein, continuous with the capillaries. Compare with arteriole.

Volar: Pertaining to the palm or sole; indicating the flexor portion of the forearm, wrist or hand.

Warfarin sodium: The sodium salt of warfarin, one of the synthetic anticoagulants. Coumadin is a brand name.

Leukocyte: Called White Blood Cells. A variety of cells within the blood and bone marrow whose general purpose is to help in fighting infection.

Whole blood: Blood from which none of the elements have been removed.

White blood cell count: The number of white blood cells (leukocytes) found in the peripheral blood and measured per cubic millimeter.

Made in the USA
Middletown, DE
31 January 2022

60128905R00091